MADAME
BOVARY

Gustave Flaubert

EDITORIAL DIRECTOR Justin Kestler
MANAGING EDITOR Ben Florman

SERIES EDITORS Boomie Aglietti, Justin Kestler
PRODUCTION Christian Lorentzen

WRITERS Margaret Miller, Brian Phillips
EDITORS John Crowther, Christian Lorentzen, Benjamin Morgan

This edition published by Spark Publishing

Spark Publishing
A Division of SparkNotes LLC
120 Fifth Avenue, 8th Floor
New York, NY 10011

02 03 04 05 SN 9 8 7 6 5 4 3 2 1

Please send all comments and questions or report errors to
feedback@sparknotes.com.

Library of Congress information available upon request

Printed and bound in the United States

RRD-C

ISBN 1-58663-442-9

INTRODUCTION: STOPPING TO BUY SPARKNOTES ON A SNOWY EVENING

Whose words these are you *think* you know.
Your paper's due tomorrow, though;
We're glad to see you stopping here
To get some help before you go.

Lost your course? You'll find it here.
Face tests and essays without fear.
Between the words, good grades at stake:
Get great results throughout the year.

Once school bells caused your heart to quake
As teachers circled each mistake.
Use SparkNotes and no longer weep,
Ace every single test you take.

Yes, books are lovely, dark, and deep,
But only what you grasp you keep,
With hours to go before you sleep,
With hours to go before you sleep.

CONTENTS

———————————————

NOTE: This SparkNote uses the Norton Critical Edition of *Madame Bovary*, edited with a substantially new translation by Paul de Man. Language and page numbering may vary in other editions.

CONTEXT

USTAVE FLAUBERT ONCE REMARKED, "Madame Bovary, c'est moi" ("Madame Bovary is me"). On the surface, this comment seems ridiculous; the circumstances of Flaubert's life have nothing in common with those he created for his most famous character. Flaubert was born in 1821 in Rouen, France. Emma Bovary's father is an uneducated farmer, whereas Flaubert's father was a respected and wealthy doctor. In addition, Emma dreams of becoming sophisticated and cosmopolitan, while Flaubert moved in the highest literary circles in Paris. Finally, Emma endures an unhappy marriage and seeks out lovers. On the contrary, the reclusive Flaubert spent most of his time living in solitude.

Since their biographies are so strikingly dissimilar, Flaubert's comment probably meant that he and his character shared many of the same struggles and desires. Emma Bovary becomes obsessed with an idealized vision of romantic love. Similarly, Flaubert became fixated at a young age upon an older woman named Elisa Schlessinger, with whom he fantasized about having a romantic relationship for many years. Emma suffers from ill health and a nervous condition; Flaubert also suffered from poor health and may have had epilepsy. Though he was an esteemed writer, Flaubert was afflicted with an abiding pessimism that caused him to sink into frequent depressions, just as Emma does when she realizes she never can have what she most desires.

Flaubert, too, could never attain what he most wanted. He remained lonely and bitter throughout his life as a writer. Though admired by his French contemporaries, Flaubert was deeply hurt by the moral outrage *Madame Bovary* provoked at its publication in 1857. The novel depicted extramarital sex in what were, for the time, graphic terms, and Flaubert and his publisher were put on trial for violation of public morals. They were acquitted, but the experience intensified Flaubert's hatred of middle-class morality.

The hatred of middle-class values is strongly apparent in *Madame Bovary*. In Flaubert's lifetime, France was caught in the throes of immense social upheaval. The Revolution of 1789 and the imperial reign of Napoleon were recent memories, and the collapse of the aristocracy was paralleled by the rise of a new middle class—

or bourgeoisie—made up of merchants and capitalists with commercial, rather than inherited, fortunes. As a member of the educated elite, Flaubert found the moral conservatism, rough manners, and unsophisticated taste of this new class appalling. He attacked the merchant class in novels such as *Madame Bovary,* the story of a woman imprisoned by her middle-class surroundings, and in another novel, *Sentimental Education.*

In addition to criticizing the middle class, Flaubert's novel also reacted against romanticism. Romantic writers, who were popular in France between the late eighteenth and mid-nineteenth centuries, wrote emotional, subjective novels that stressed feeling at the expense of facts and reason. When Flaubert began writing, a new school called realism had started challenging romantic idealism with books that focused on the harsh realities of life. This school included other French writers such as Stendhal and Honorè Balzac, as well as English writers like George Eliot and Thomas Hardy. Unlike his contemporaries, however, Flaubert recognized a strong streak of romanticism in himself. In *Madame Bovary,* romanticism is present, but Flaubert always treats it with irony. Flaubert allows himself a few romantic moments but recognizes their flaws.

Though it was his first novel, *Madame Bovary* is Flaubert's most accomplished and admired work. In many ways, the novel provides the blueprint for the genre of the modern novel. For example, Flaubert was a pioneering stylist, matching the style of his prose to the action of his story in a remarkable new way. Where other realist novels of the mid-nineteenth century used detached, objective narration, Flaubert's prose conveys the mood of his characters. When Emma is bored and restless, the prose plods dully; when she experiences sensual pleasure, it moves rapturously and swiftly. We frequently see this technique of communicating mood through language in novels today.

Plot Overview

MADAME BOVARY begins when Charles Bovary is a young boy, unable to fit in at his new school and ridiculed by his new classmates. As a child, and later when he grows into a young man, Charles is mediocre and dull. He fails his first medical exam and only barely manages to become a second-rate country doctor. His mother marries him off to a widow who dies soon afterward, leaving Charles much less money than he expected.

Charles soon falls in love with Emma, the daughter of a patient, and the two decide to marry. After an elaborate wedding, they set up house in Tostes, where Charles has his practice. But marriage doesn't live up to Emma's romantic expectations. Ever since she lived in a convent as a young girl, she has dreamed of love and marriage as a solution to all her problems. After she attends an extravagant ball at the home of a wealthy nobleman, she begins to dream constantly of a more sophisticated life. She grows bored and depressed when she compares her fantasies to the humdrum reality of village life, and eventually her listlessness makes her ill. When Emma becomes pregnant, Charles decides to move to a different town in hopes of reviving her health.

In the new town of Yonville, the Bovarys meet Homais, the town pharmacist, a pompous windbag who loves to hear himself speak. Emma also meets Leon, a law clerk, who, like her, is bored with rural life and loves to escape through romantic novels. When Emma gives birth to her daughter Berthe, motherhood disappoints her— she had desired a son—and she continues to be despondent. Romantic feelings blossom between Emma and Leon. However, when Emma realizes that Leon loves her, she feels guilty and throws herself into the role of a dutiful wife. Leon grows tired of waiting and, believing that he can never possess Emma, departs to study law in Paris. His departure makes Emma miserable.

Soon, at an agricultural fair, a wealthy neighbor named Rodolphe, who is attracted by Emma's beauty, declares his love to her. He seduces her, and they begin having a passionate affair. Emma is often indiscreet, and the townspeople all gossip about her. Charles, however, suspects nothing. His adoration for his wife and his stupidity combine to blind him to her indiscretions. His professional reputation, meanwhile, suffers a severe blow when he and Homais attempt an experimental surgical technique to treat a club-footed man named Hippolyte and end up having to call in another doctor to amputate the leg. Disgusted with her husband's incompetence, Emma throws herself even more passionately into her affair with Rodolphe. She borrows money to buy him gifts and suggests that they run off together and take little Berthe with them. Soon enough, though, the jaded and worldly Rodolphe has grown bored of Emma's demanding affections. Refusing to elope with her, he leaves her. Heartbroken, Emma grows desperately ill and nearly dies.

By the time Emma recovers, Charles is in financial trouble from having to borrow money to pay off Emma's debts and to pay for her treatment. Still, he decides to take Emma to the opera in the nearby city of Rouen. There, they encounter Leon. This meeting rekindles the old romantic flame between Emma and Leon, and this time the two embark on a love affair. As Emma continues sneaking off to Rouen to meet Leon, she also grows deeper and deeper in debt to the moneylender Lheureux, who lends her more and more money at exaggerated interest rates. She grows increasingly careless in conducting her affair with Leon. As a result, on several occasions, her acquaintances nearly discover her infidelity.

Over time, Emma grows bored with Leon. Not knowing how to abandon him, she instead becomes increasingly demanding. Meanwhile, her debts mount daily. Eventually, Lheureux orders the seizure of Emma's property to compensate for the debt she has accumulated. Terrified of Charles finding out, she frantically tries to raise the money that she needs, appealing to Leon and to all the town's businessmen. Eventually, she even attempts to prostitute herself by offering to get back together with Rodolphe if he will give her the money she needs. He refuses, and, driven to despair, she commits suicide by eating arsenic. She dies in horrible agony.

For a while, Charles idealizes the memory of his wife. Eventually, though, he finds her letters from Rodolphe and Leon, and he is forced to confront the truth. He dies alone in his garden, and Berthe is sent off to work in a cotton mill.

CHARACTER LIST

Emma Bovary The novel's protagonist, the Madame Bovary of
the title. A country girl educated in a convent and
married to Charles Bovary at a young age, she harbors
idealistic romantic illusions, covets sophistication,
sensuality, and passion, and lapses into fits of extreme
boredom and depression when her life fails to match
the sentimental novels she treasures. She has a
daughter, Berthe, but lacks maternal instincts and is
often annoyed with the child. Occasionally, guilt or a
memory of her simple childhood causes her to repent,
and she becomes devoutly religious and dedicates
herself to her husband and child. Such fits of conscience
are short-lived. Emma's desire for passion and pleasure
leads her into extramarital affairs with Rodolphe and
Leon. In addition, she runs up enormous debts against
her husband's property and commits suicide when she
realizes she will be unable to repay them.

Charles Bovary A country doctor, kind, but simple, dull, and
unremarkable. Charles is a terrible doctor who
manages simple cases decently but is incapable of
performing difficult operations. For example, when he
tries to operate on Hippolyte's leg, it develops gangrene
and has to be removed. Charles dotes on his wife,
Emma, who can do no wrong in his eyes. Only his
mother holds as much sway over him as his wife, and
even she loses control over him after his marriage.
Despite his deep love for Emma, he doesn't understand
her. Her looks and dress captivate him, but he remains
oblivious to her personality. His adoration of her often
leads him to act with baffling innocence. He fails to
detect her extramarital affairs with Rodolphe and
Leon, which are so poorly concealed that they become
the subjects of town gossip. When Emma begins to run

up debts, he grants her power of attorney over all his property, an act that leads to his financial ruin. After Emma's suicide, he learns of her infidelities and, soon after, dies a broken man.

Monsieur Homais The apothecary at Yonville; a pompous, self-impressed man of the bourgeois class who helps Charles become established as a doctor in the town. Homais is superficial and obnoxious. He loves to hear himself talk, and his lengthy commentaries are filled with clichés. His pomposity can cause real harm, as when he encourages Charles to operate on Hippolyte to disastrous effect. An irreligious man, Homais often argues with Bournisien, the town priest, claiming that religion and prayer are useless. Homais is the perfect embodiment of all the bourgeois values and characteristics that so disgust Flaubert and bore his heroine, Emma.

Leon Emma's friend in Yonville, who later becomes her lover. When Leon is a law clerk in Yonville, he shares many of Emma's romantic preconceptions and her love for sentimental novels. He falls in love with her but moves away to Paris to study law, partly because he considers their love impossible as long as she remains married. When Emma meets him later in Rouen, his time in the city has made him more sure of himself. He now perceives Emma to be unsophisticated and thinks he can win her love. Although Emma believes him to be cosmopolitan, Flaubert presents him as awkward and full of himself. Drawn to his newfound urban sophistication, Emma begins an affair with him. At first, they succeed in living up to one another's romantic ideals. However, as the affair progresses, Emma and Leon grow increasingly bored and disgusted with one another. He cannot help her when she is in monetary distress and makes excuses for failing to help her financially. Leon marries shortly after Emma's death.

Rodolphe Boulanger Emma's first lover, a wealthy landowner with an estate near Yonville. Rodolphe is shrewd, selfish, and manipulative. He has had scores of lovers and believes Emma to be no more sincere than any of them. He plots his seduction of Emma with strategic precision, begins an affair with her, and then abandons her when he becomes bored of her romantic fancies and emotional demands.

Monsieur Lheureux A sly, sinister merchant and moneylender in Yonville who leads Emma into debt, financial ruin, and eventually suicide by playing on her weakness for luxury and extravagance. Lheureux is a bit of a devil figure who tempts people with luxuries they can't afford and knows just when to appear with his requests for money and promises of more loans.

Abbé Bournisien The town priest in Yonville, Bournisien tends to focus more on worldly matters than on spiritual ones. He often argues with Homais about the value of religion, but seems incapable of grasping deep spiritual problems.

Hippolyte The crippled servant at the inn in Yonville. Under pressure from Emma and Homais, Charles attempts to operate on Hippolyte's club foot. The operation fails, gangrene sets in, and Hippolyte loses his leg.

Berthe Charles and Emma's daughter, who is condemned to a life of poverty by her mother's financial excesses and her parents' deaths.

Binet The tax collector in Yonville. Binet takes his meals regularly at the Lion d'Or inn. He is quiet, and amuses himself by making napkin rings on the lathe in his attic.

Guillaumin Leon's first employer, the well-to-do lawyer in Yonville. When Emma seeks his help with her financial hardship, he offers his assistance in return for sexual favors—an offer she angrily declines.

Rouault   Emma's father, a simple, essentially kindly farmer with a weakness for drink. He is devoted both to Emma and to the memory of his first wife, whom he loved deeply.

Lariviere   An esteemed doctor from Rouen who is called in after Emma takes arsenic at the end of the novel. He is coldly analytical and condescending to his inferiors, but he is brilliant and competent, and he feels a real sympathy for his patients.

The elder Madame Bovary A bitter, conservative woman who spoiled her son Charles as a youth and disapproves of his marriage to Emma. She sees through Emma's lies and tries to get Charles to rein in his wife's excessive spending, but she rarely succeeds.

Justin   Homais's assistant. Justin is young, impressionable, and simple. He falls terribly in love with Emma and unwittingly gives her access to the arsenic that she uses to commit suicide.

Heloise Dubuc Charles's first wife. She realizes that Charles is enamored with Emma. Soon after having this realization, she dies from the shock of having all her property stolen by her lawyer.

ANALYSIS OF MAJOR CHARACTERS

EMMA BOVARY

In Emma Bovary, Flaubert uses irony to criticize romanticism and to investigate the relation of beauty to corruption and of fate to free will. Emma embarks directly down a path to moral and financial ruin over the course of the novel. She is very beautiful, as we can tell by the way several men fall in love with her, but she is morally corrupt and unable to accept and appreciate the realities of her life. Since her girlhood in a convent, she has read romantic novels that feed her discontent with her ordinary life. She dreams of the purest, most impossible forms of love and wealth, ignoring whatever beauty is present in the world around her. Flaubert once said, "Madame Bovary is me," and many scholars believe that he was referring to a weakness he shared with his character for romance, sentimental flights of fancy, and melancholy. Flaubert, however, approaches romanticism with self-conscious irony, pointing out its flaws even as he is tempted by it. Emma, on the other hand, never recognizes that her desires are unreasonable. She rails emotionally against the society that, from her perspective, makes them impossible for her to achieve.

Emma's failure is not completely her own. Her character demonstrates the many ways in which circumstance—rather than free will—determined the position of women in the nineteenth century. If Emma were as rich as her lover, Rodolphe, for instance, she would be free to indulge the lifestyle she imagines. Flaubert suggests at times that her dissatisfaction with the bourgeois society she lives in is justified. For example, the author includes details that seem to ridicule Homais's pompous speechmaking or Charles's boorish table manners. These details indicate that Emma's plight is emblematic of the difficulties of any sensitive person trapped among the French bourgeoisie. But Emma's inability to accept her situation and her attempt to escape it through adultery and deception constitute moral errors. These mistakes bring about her ruin and, in the process, cause harm to innocent people around her. For example, though dim-witted and unable to recognize his wife's true character, Charles loves Emma, and she deceives him. Similarly, little Berthe is but an innocent child in need of her mother's care and love, but Emma is cold to her, and Berthe ends up working in a cotton mill because of Emma's selfish spending and suicide, and because of Charles's resulting death.

We can see that Emma's role as a woman may have an even greater effect on the course of her life than her social status does. Emma is frequently portrayed as the object of a man's gaze: her husband's, Rodolphe's, Leon's, Justin's—even Flaubert's, since the whole novel is essentially a description of how he sees Emma. Moreover, Emma's only power over the men in her life is sexual. Near the end of her life, when she searches desperately for money, she has to ask men for it, and the only thing she can use to persuade them to give it to her is sex. Emma's prostitution is the result of her self-destructive spending, but the fact that, as a woman, she has no other means of finding money is a result of the misogynistic society in which she lives.

CHARLES BOVARY

Charles represents both the society and the personal characteristics that Emma detests. He is incompetent, stupid, and unimaginative. In one of the novel's most revelatory moments, Charles looks into Emma's eyes and sees not her soul but rather his own image, reflected in miniature. Charles's perception of his own reflection is not narcissistic but merely a simple, direct sensation, unmediated by romantic notions. The moment demonstrates his inability to imagine an idealized version of the world or find mystic qualities in the world's physical aspects. Instead, he views life literally and never imbues what he sees with romantic import. Thus it is the physical aspects of Emma that delight Charles. When the narrative focuses on his point of view, we see every detail of her dress, her skin, and her hair. When it comes to her aspirations and depressions, however, Charles is at a loss. He nods and smiles dumbly as Emma conducts the same sorts of conversations with him that she does with her dog. Charles is too stupid to manage his money well or to see through Emma's obvious lies, and he is a frighteningly incompetent doctor. In one scene, as he goes to repair Rouault's leg, we learn that he is trying desperately to "call to mind all the fractures he [knows]." His operation on Hippolyte's clubfoot, while it is not his idea, is a complete failure. Charles is more than merely incompetent, however. He is physically repulsive, though it's hard to tell from Flaubert's descriptions whether he is actually an ugly man or whether he appears disgusting only through Emma's eyes.

Despite his unimaginative nature, Charles is one of the novel's most moral and sincere characters. He truly loves Emma, forgiving her even when he finally recognizes her infidelities. He does everything he can to save her when she is ill, and he gives her the benefit of the doubt whenever her lies seem to fail her. Literal-minded, humble, free of temptations, and without aspirations, Charles is Emma's opposite. While she possesses some beauty, sensitivity, and intelligence despite her moral corruption, Charles remains good-hearted despite his boorishness and stupidity.

MONSIEUR HOMAIS

Although Homais is not central to the plot of *Madame Bovary*, he is an absolutely essential part of its atmosphere. He is a pompous speechmaker, endlessly rattling on about medical techniques and theories that he really knows nothing about. His presence serves, in part, to heighten our sense of Emma's frustration with her life. Flaubert relates Homais's speeches in full, forcing us to read them just as Emma is forced to listen to them. Homais is also an extremely selfish man. When the Bovarys first arrive in Yonville, we learn that he is only befriending Charles because he wants Charles to turn a blind eye to his disreputable medical practices.

In the last sentence of the book, Homais receives the Legion of Honor, a medal he has always dreamed of attaining, after Emma and Charles are both dead. Meanwhile, Charles—who loved his wife as deeply as he was capable—and Emma—who yearned to live an exceptional life—are both punished. By rewarding Homais, Flaubert does not advocate his kind of life. Instead, he shows us a realistic portrayal of one of the most disappointing aspects of the world—that the mediocre and the selfish often fare better than either those who live passionately and try to be exceptional or those who live humbly and treat others with kind generosity.

THEMES, MOTIFS & SYMBOLS

THEMES

Themes are the fundamental and often universal ideas explored in a literary work.

THE INADEQUACY OF LANGUAGE

Madame Bovary explores the possibility that the written word fails to capture even a small part of the depth of a human life. Flaubert uses a variety of techniques to show how language is often an inadequate medium for expressing emotions and ideas. The characters' frequent inability to communicate with each other is emblematic of the fact that words do not perfectly describe what they signify. In the first chapter, for example, Charles's teacher thinks he says his name is "Charbovari." He fails to make his own name understood. This inadequacy of speech is something Emma will encounter again and again as she tries to make her distress known to the priest or to express her love to Rodolphe. It is also present when Charles reads the letter from Rodolphe and misinterprets it as a note of platonic affection.

The lies that fill *Madame Bovary* contribute to the sense of language's inadequacy in the novel, and to the notion that words may be more effective for the purposes of obscuring the truth or conveying its opposite, than for representing the truth itself. Emma's life is described as "a tissue of lies." She invents story after story to prevent her husband from discovering her affairs. Similarly, Rodolphe tells so many lies about his love for Emma that he assumes her words are also insincere. Flaubert points out that by lying the lovers make it impossible for words ever to touch at the truth in things.

The strong sense of the inadequacy of language is in part a reaction against the school of realism. Although Flaubert was in some senses a realist, he also believed it was wrong to claim that realism provided a more accurate picture of life than romanticism. He deploys ironic romantic descriptions to establish a tension between various characters' experience of events and the real aspects of life.

By combining ironic romanticism and literal realistic narration, Flaubert captures his characters and their struggles mormore fully than a strictly literal or a wholesale romantic style would allow.

THE POWERLESSNESS OF WOMEN

Emma Bovary's hope that her baby will be a man because "a woman is always hampered" is just one of the many instances in the novel in which Flaubert demonstrates an intimate understanding of the plight of women in his time. We see throughout *Madame Bovary* how Emma's male companions possess the power to change her life for better or worse—a power that she herself lacks. Even Charles contributes to Emma's powerlessness. His laziness prevents him from becoming a good doctor, and his incompetence prevents him from advancing into a higher social stratum that might satisfy Emma's yearnings. As a result, Emma is stuck in a country town without much money. Rodolphe, who possesses the financial power to whisk Emma away from her life, abandons her, and, as a woman, she is incapable of fleeing on her own. Leon at first seems similar to Emma. Both are discontented with country life, and both dream of bigger and better things. But because Leon is a man, he has the power to actually fulfill his dream of moving to the city, whereas Emma must stay in Yonville, shackled to a husband and child.

Ultimately, however, the novel's moral structure requires that Emma assume responsibility for her own actions. She can't blame everything on the men around her. She freely chooses to be unfaithful to Charles, and her infidelities wound him fatally in the end. On the other hand, in Emma's situation, the only two choices she has are to take lovers or to remain faithful in a dull marriage. Once she has married Charles, the choice to commit adultery is Emma's only means of exercising power over her own destiny. While men have access to wealth and property, the only currency Emma possesses to influence others is her body, a form of capital she can trade only in secret with the price of shame and the added expense of deception. When she pleads desperately for money to pay her debts, men offer the money in return for sexual favors. Eventually, she tries to win back Rodolphe as a lover if he will pay her debts. Even her final act of suicide is made possible by a transaction funded with her physical charms, which are dispensed toward Justin, who allows Emma access to the cupboard where the arsenic is kept. Even to take her own life, she must resort to sexual power, using Justin's love for her to convince him to do what she wants.

THE FAILURES OF THE BOURGEOISIE

Emma's disappointments stem in great part from her dissatisfaction with the world of the French bourgeoisie. She aspires to have taste that is more refined and sophisticated than that of her class. This frustration reflects a rising social and historical trend of the last half of the nineteenth century. At the time Flaubert was writing, the word "bourgeois" referred to the middle class: people who lacked the independent wealth and ancestry of the nobility, but whose professions did not require them to perform physical labor to earn their living. Their tastes were characterized as gaudily materialistic. They indulged themselves as their means allowed, but without discrimination. The mediocrity of the bourgeoisie was frustrating to Flaubert, and he used Emma Bovary's disgust with her class as a way of conveying his own hatred for the middle class. *Madame Bovary* shows how ridiculous, stifling, and potentially harmful the attitudes and trappings of the bourgeoisie can be. In the pharmacist Homais's long-winded, know-it-all speeches, Flaubert mocks the bourgeois class's pretensions to knowledge and learning and its faith in the power of technologies that it doesn't completely understand. But Homais is not just funny; he is also dangerous. When he urges Charles to try a new medical procedure on Hippolyte, the patient acquires gangrene and then loses his leg. Homais does even greater damage when he attempts to treat Emma for her poisoning. He tries to show off by analyzing the poison and coming up with an antidote. Later, a doctor will tell him that he should have simply stuck a finger down Emma's throat to save her life.

MOTIFS

Motifs are recurring structures, contrasts, or literary devices that can help to develop and inform the text's major themes.

DEATH AND ILLNESS

There are many disturbing references to death and illness in *Madame Bovary,* and the novel can seem very morbid. These references emphasize Flaubert's realistic, unflinching description of the world, and also act as physical manifestations of Emma's moral decay. For example, Lestiboudois grows potatoes in the graveyard because the decomposing bodies help them grow, and Homais keeps fetuses in jars. Similarly, Hippolyte loses his leg to gangrene, the blind beggar with festering skin follows the carriage to and from

Rouen, and, when Emma faints in Part Two, Chapter XIII, Homais wakes her up with smelling salts, saying, "this thing would resuscitate a corpse!" Such excessive corruption is a comment on the physical state of the world. Flaubert constantly reminds us that death and decay lurk beneath the surface of everyday life, and that innocence is often coupled very closely with corruption. This focus on the negative aspects of life is part of Flaubert's realism.

WINDOWS

Windows are frequently associated with Emma. We often see her looking out of them, or we glimpse her through them from the street as she waves goodbye to Charles or Leon. For Emma, these windows represent the possibility of escape. A shutter bangs open to announce her engagement, and she contemplates jumping out the attic window to commit suicide. But Emma never manages to really escape. She stays inside the window, looking out at the world and imagining a freedom that she never can obtain. Windows also serve to take Emma back to the past. At the ball, when the servant breaks the window and Emma sees the peasants outside, she is suddenly reminded of her simple childhood. Such a retreat to childhood also could be a kind of escape for Emma, who would surely be much happier if she stopped striving to escape that simple life. But, again, she ignores the possibility of escape, trapping herself within her own desires for romantic ideals of wealth she can't obtain.

EATING

The quantity of food consumed in *Madame Bovary* could feed an army for a week. From Emma's wedding feast to the Bovarys' daily dinner, Flaubert's characters are frequently eating, and the way they eat reveals important character traits. Charles's atrocious table manners, magnified through Emma's disgust, reveal him to be boorish and lacking in sophistication. When Emma is shown sucking her fingers or licking out the bottom of a glass, we see a base animal sensuality and a lust for physical satisfaction in her that all her pretensions to refinement cannot conceal. Finally, when Emma goes to the ball, the exquisite table manners of the nobles and the fine foods they consume signify the refinement and sophistication of their class. In each of these cases, what one eats or how one eats is an indicator of social class.

SYMBOLS

Symbols are objects, characters, figures, or colors used to represent abstract ideas or concepts.

THE BLIND BEGGAR

A picture of physical decay, the blind beggar who follows the carriage in which Emma rides to meet Leon also symbolizes Emma's moral corruption. He sings songs about "birds and sunshine and green leaves" in a voice "like an inarticulate lament of some vague despair." This coupling of innocence with disease relates to the combination of beauty and corruption that Emma herself has become. While her words, appearance, and fantasies are those of an innocent and beautiful wife, her spirit becomes foul and corrupt as she indulges herself in adulterous temptations and the deceptions required to maintain her illicit affairs. Later, when Emma dies, the blind man gets to the end of his song about a young girl dreaming. We then discover that what we thought was a song about an innocent woman is actually a bawdy, sexual song. This progression from innocence to sexual degradation mirrors the path of Emma's life.

DRIED FLOWERS

When Emma comes home with Charles, she notices his dead wife's wedding bouquet in the bedroom and wonders what will happen to her own bouquet when she dies. Later, when they move to Yonville, she burns her own bouquet as a gesture of defiance against her unhappy marriage. The dried bouquet stands for disappointed hopes, and for the new promise of a wedding day turned sour and old. In another sense, Emma's burning of her bouquet foreshadows the way her desires will consume her youth and, eventually, her life.

THE LATHE

Binet's habit of making useless napkin rings on his lathe is a symbol with several meanings. First, it represents the useless, nonproductive, ornamental character of bourgeois tastes. Second, it represents something more ominous—the monotony of the life that traps Emma. In the scene in which she contemplates throwing herself out the window, Emma hears the sound of the lathe calling her to suicide. Finally, the lathe represents the craftsman repeatedly making a simple, uniform work of art. Flaubert once compared himself as a writer to a craftsman working on a lathe.

Summary & Analysis

Part One, Chapters I–III

Summary: Chapter I

The novel begins at the village school, where a new student has just arrived. He is Charles Bovary, the son of a former army surgeon and his wife, who lives on a small farm. After observing Charles on his first day at school, we follow him as he grows up. Charles's father, who manages money poorly and philanders with "all the village harlots," has long since lost the respect of his wife, who lavishes her effusive affections on Charles instead. Despite the ridiculous way she spoils him, Charles remains an unremarkable child—good-natured, but lazy and unimaginative. Eventually, his parents send him off to medical school, where he regularly skips classes and plays dominoes instead of studying. His laziness causes him to fail his first attempt at the medical exam, a failure concealed from his father until years later. After retaking the exam, he passes and becomes a doctor. His mother arranges for him to practice in the village of Tostes. She also finds him a wife—Heloise Dubuc, a wealthy widow, years older than Charles. Heloise gives Charles little love but plenty of nagging and scolding.

Summary: Chapter II

One night, Charles is called from his bed at 4 A.M. to set a simple fracture at a distant farm. He admires the patient's daughter, a young woman named Emma, who was raised in a convent and is unhappy with country life. Struck by her beauty, he returns to visit her father, Rouault, far more often than necessary while his leg heals. Heloise grows suspicious and asks around about Rouault's daughter, who, she hears, is prone to putting on airs. Jealous of Emma's looks and good breeding, Heloise forces Charles to promise never to go there again. He agrees but learns soon after that Heloise's lawyer has stolen most of Heloise's money, and that Heloise lied about her wealth before the wedding. Charles's parents argue violently about this development, and Heloise, shocked and humiliated, dies suddenly, a week later.

SUMMARY: CHAPTER III

After Heloise's death, Charles befriends Rouault and often visits his farm. He spends time with Emma, watching her work or chatting with her about her boredom in the country. Although he pays no attention to the meaning of her words, Charles soon finds himself in love with Emma, and Rouault, a heavy drinker who has mismanaged his farm, agrees to give his daughter to this meek but kind and well-mannered physician. After consenting, Rouault instructs Charles to wait outside while he goes to the house to ask Emma. He alerts Charles to her agreement with a pre-arranged signal, a shutter banged against the wall. The couple must wait for Charles's mourning period to pass. They bide the time planning the wedding. Emma wants a romantic midnight wedding, but in the end she is forced to settle for a more traditional ceremony, with raucous celebration.

ANALYSIS: PART ONE, CHAPTERS I–III

The novel's early chapters set the middle-class provincial scene and introduce the fundamental elements of Emma's and Charles's characters. Charles's failure to pass his medical exams and his inability to comprehend Emma's words illustrate his dullness and complacency, and his awareness of the tiny details of her physical beauty betray that he thinks of her more as an object than as a person. For her part, Emma possesses an impractical, romantic, melancholy nature—she hopes for a torch-lit midnight wedding—which even at this early stage seems at odds with the realities of her life.

Madame Bovary does not begin its narrative focused on Madame Bovary, and, throughout the first few chapters, Flaubert delays the introduction of the novel's heroine. Flaubert's use of narrative perspective in these chapters keeps his reader waiting for a glimpse of his heroine, Emma. It's almost as if Flaubert makes us penetrate through several layers of perspective before we are allowed to see through Emma's eyes. The first scene in the book is told in the first-person plural. "We" are Charles's classmates observing his bumbling arrival at his new school. Soon afterward, this narrative voice fades into the background and Flaubert begins to use the third person, restricting most of his observations to Charles's point of view. At first, Charles seems to be the protagonist of the story. Emma seems somewhat peripheral, and we learn about her only through other characters' perceptions. Charles finds her charming, and Heloise has heard that she puts on airs.

The novel introduces two Madames Bovary before Emma: Charles's mother and his first wife. The relations between these women and Charles prefigure his relations with the "Madame Bovary" of the title. Both Charles's domineering mother and his first wife render him a man who expects to be controlled. The Madames Bovary differ from Emma. Whereas, like Charles himself, the first two Madames Bovary are petty and unimaginative, Emma longs for a grand, romantic life. In that sense, she has a hard time filling the shoes of either Charles's mother or his dead wife, while her own qualities are beyond Charles's powers of comprehension.

PART ONE, CHAPTERS IV–VI

SUMMARY: CHAPTER IV
In spring, when Charles's mourning period for his first wife has ended, he marries Emma. The wedding is a huge event all around Rouault's farm, and the guests come dressed in fancy clothes that they are not used to. After the wedding, they all return to the farm in a long and festive procession that stretches out "like one long coloured scarf that undulated across the fields." They consume a massive all-night feast that includes an incredibly elaborate three-tiered wedding cake. The next day, after the wedding night, Charles is obviously overjoyed. Emma takes her loss of virginity calmly and coolly in stride. As the couple departs for their home in Tostes, Rouault reminisces about the happiness of his own wedding day.

SUMMARY: CHAPTER V
Back in Tostes, Emma inspects her new home, where she makes Charles remove his dead wife's dried bridal bouquet from the bedroom. As Emma plans further small improvements to the house, Charles dotes on her in a daze of love and happiness. Emma, on the other hand, feels strangely dissatisfied by her new life—she always expected marriage to lead her to romantic bliss. Instead, she feels that her life has fallen short of the high expectations she received from romantic novels: "Before marriage she thought herself in love; but since the happiness that should have followed failed to come, she must, she thought, have been mistaken. And Emma tried to find out what one meant exactly in life by the words *bliss, passion, ecstasy,* that had seemed to her so beautiful in books."

SUMMARY: CHAPTER VI

Emma remembers life in the convent where she was educated. At
first, she threw herself into religious life, treating religion with the
same passion she devoted to reading romantic novels and listening
to ballads of love. When her mother died, she immersed herself even
more passionately into her grief. It pleased her to think of herself as
an example of pure melancholy. But she soon grew tired of mourning and eventually left the convent. For a while, she enjoyed life on
her father's farm, but she soon found herself bored and disgusted
with her life. In this state of disillusionment, she first met Charles,
but he did not provide the happy escape for which she had hoped.

ANALYSIS: PART ONE, CHAPTERS IV–VI

Flaubert's shifting of the point of view from character to character
follows the pattern of the novel's plot. After Charles marries Emma,
her point of view takes over. This shift in perspective begins at the
end of Chapter V and coincides with the contrast between Charles's
blind love for Emma and her own disillusionment. In Emma's med-
itation on her marital dissatisfaction, we catch our first real glimpse
of her thoughts, and the stage is set for the escalating crisis of personality that will eventually claim her life.

A third-person narrator tells the story throughout most of
Madame Bovary, focusing primarily on Emma's thoughts and
actions. However, the narrator's point of view does change, and the
narrator adopts several different tones. The narrator frequently
speaks as an outsider, commenting objectively, but also shows us
things subjectively through the characters' eyes, telling us what they
feel and think. Flaubert often employs free indirect discourse, a
technique in which the narrator's words sound very much like the
thoughts and speech patterns of one of the characters, even when
the narrator is not directly quoting the character. For example,
when Rouault remembers his wedding in Chapter IV, Flaubert
writes, "How long ago it all was! Their son would have been thirty
by now. Then he looked back and saw nothing on the road." The
narration moves directly from transcription of Rouault's thought to
description of his action, without setting the thought apart in quotation marks. As a result, we must often stop to consider whether we
are hearing the voice of the narrator or that of a character.

One of Emma's most important characteristics is the conflict
between her romantic nature and her tendency toward discontent.

Emma's flashback shows how far back her taste for romance extends. Even at age thirteen, she was unable to resist the melancholy, romantic atmosphere of the convent and steeped herself in romantic novels and songs, whose stories she desperately wished would be realized in her own life. Emma, however, is easily discontented. Things that she believes will save her, such as the convent, the farm, and married life, always fail to fulfill her desires. Her high spirits after the wedding, for instance, fall the moment she encounters Heloise's bridal bouquet in Charles's house, and she immediately begins to wonder why her life does not match the sentimental fictions she had expected to come true.

Flaubert is often considered a realist writer. Realists challenged their romantic predecessors by writing books that focused on the details of everyday life without turning a blind eye to their dreary aspects. Flaubert participates in this movement by describing his characters' emotions, actions, and settings vividly and without romantic or fantastic embellishment. The wedding scene that takes up almost all of Chapter IV is a classic example of what makes Flaubert a realist. The wedding is a setting that Flaubert describes painstakingly. He writes about every part of the celebration, often merely listing item after item. He tells what kinds of vehicles the guests arrive in, how they wear their hair, what fabrics their clothes are made of, and how they appear physically. His description of the feast is so elaborate that it seems like there's far too much food for just forty-three guests to eat. Flaubert doesn't just rattle off details. He also implicitly comments on their social value. When he tells us about the young girls, "their hair greasy with rose-pomade, and very much afraid of dirtying their gloves," we can see how awkward and unrefined they are. In describing the country people's attempts to dress up, Flaubert pokes fun at their efforts.

Such subtle commentary on the traits of minor characters is just one of the ways in which Flaubert frames *Madame Bovary* as a critical portrait of bourgeois life. In Chapter VI, he writes that Emma loves the flowers and icons of her religion, but that real spiritual faith is "alien to her constitution." This statement shows that Emma, for all her pretensions to great sentiment, is really incapable of deep feeling. The narrator's remark also satirizes bourgeois churchgoers who make a great show of religion but possess little genuine piety.

PART ONE, CHAPTERS VII–IX

[A]ll the bitterness of life seemed to be served to her on her plate. . . .

(See QUOTATIONS, p. 51)

SUMMARY: CHAPTER VII

During her honeymoon in Tostes, Emma feels disappointed not to be in a romantic chalet in Switzerland. She finds her husband dull and uninspiring and begins to resent his lack of interest in a more passionate life. Charles continues to love Emma. His mother visits and hates Emma for having won his love. After she leaves, Emma tries to love Charles, but disappointment lingers. She wonders why she ever got married. Then, one of Charles's patients, the Marquis d'Andervilliers, invites the Bovarys to a ball at his mansion.

SUMMARY: CHAPTER VIII

Although enchanted by the atmosphere of wealth and luxury at the ball, Emma is embarrassed by her husband, whom she views as a clumsy, unsophisticated oaf. She is surrounded by wealthy, elegant noblemen and women, among them an old man who was one of Marie Antoinette's lovers. When the ballroom gets too hot, a servant breaks the windows to let in the air. Emma looks outside and sees peasants gawking in; she is reminded of her life on the farm, which now feels a world away. A viscount dances with her, and she feels as though she has been cheated out of the life for which she was born. On the way home, the same viscount passes them on the road and drops a cigar box, which Emma keeps. Back in Tostes, Emma is angry with everyone around her.

SUMMARY: CHAPTER IX

Fixated on her cigar case and her fashionable ladies' magazines, Emma sinks into fantasies of high society life in Paris, growing despondent and miserable and venting her self-pity by acting sullen and capricious with her husband. Although Charles's business prospers, Emma grows increasingly irritated with his poor manners and dullness. As her restlessness, boredom, and depression intensify, she becomes physically ill. In an effort to cure her, Charles decides that they should move to Yonville, a town in need of a doctor. Before the move, Emma learns that she is pregnant. While packing, she throws her dried bridal bouquet into the fire and watches it burn.

ANALYSIS: PART ONE, CHAPTERS VII–IX

Now that we see the world of the novel fully from Emma's perspective, Flaubert begins to develop the basic conflict inherent in her situation: Emma is unable to accept the world as it is, but she cannot make the world as she wants it to be. Now that she is married to a middle-class dullard, she cannot accept her lot. She steeps herself in fantasy, and the pressure of her constant rebellion against reality makes her restless, moody, and eventually physically ill.

Flaubert's portrayal of the ball and the events that follow displays the ironic contrast between Emma's experience and reality. Flaubert conveys both the external reality of how Emma looks at the ball as well the psychological reality of how the ball looks to Emma. She is so happy that she fails to realize that no one at the ball is paying any attention to her, and her meaningless dance with the viscount becomes, in her fancy, a tremendous romantic occurrence. In fact, she continues to overlook the well-meaning love of her good-natured but vapid husband in favor of her memories of the ball for weeks after everyone else has already forgotten it. When Charles decides to move to Yonville in an attempt to salvage Emma's failing health, she takes a moment from her packing to throw her bridal wreath dramatically onto the fire. The event symbolizes her rejection of the marriage and the complacent middle-class world that have, to her mind, imprisoned her.

Emma's prejudiced eyes intensify Flaubert's realist attention to detail. In particular, the details of Charles's oafishness are greatly magnified. The narrator describes every noise he makes when he eats. Flaubert also devotes several paragraphs to a description of Emma's overwhelmingly boring daily routine. Emma's boredom becomes one of the novel's subjects and a means of developing her character. Flaubert's focus on boredom marks another of the novel's departures from romanticism toward a realistic mode.

Emma's relation to her farming roots is also explored in this section. Flaubert places a recollection of the past in the middle of Emma's fantasy evening to show that she can never really escape her origins. At the ball, Emma allows herself to forget that she is not a privileged member of the upper-class world she is visiting, but when a servant breaks a windowpane, Emma sees the peasants outside, and she remembers the simple country life of her youth.

PART TWO, CHAPTERS I–III

> *She hoped for a son; he would be strong and dark; she would call him George; and this idea of having a male child was like an expected revenge for all her impotence in the past.*
>
> (See QUOTATIONS, p. 52)

SUMMARY: CHAPTER I

Part Two begins with a description of Yonville-l'Abbaye, the town to which the Bovarys are moving. The most notable features of the town are the Lion d'Or inn, the pharmacy of Monsieur Homais, and the graveyard, where the gravedigger, Lestiboudois, also grows potatoes. The village folk await the arrival of the evening coach. It arrives late, carrying Charles and Emma. The delay has occured because Emma's little dog escaped and ran away during the journey.

SUMMARY: CHAPTER II

Charles's correspondent in Yonville, a pompous, obnoxious apothecary named Homais, dines at the inn with the newly arrived Bovarys. His boarder, a young law clerk named Leon, is invited to join them. While Charles and Homais discuss medicine, Emma and Leon spend much of the meal discovering their affinities. Emma learns that Leon also loves romantic novels and lofty ideals. Sharing these leanings, the two feel an immediate closeness and believe that their conversation is quite profound. When the Bovarys arrive at their new house, Emma hopes that her life will change for the better, and that her unhappiness will finally subside.

SUMMARY: CHAPTER III

Leon thinks about Emma constantly. Charles's medical practice gets off to a slow start, but Charles is excited about the coming of the baby. Finally, the baby is born. It is a girl, contrary to Emma's wishes. They name her Berthe, and Charles's parents stay with them for a month after the christening party. One day, Emma decides to visit the baby at the house of her wet nurse, who asks her for a few extra amenities. On the way there, Emma feels weak, so she asks Leon to accompany her. Rumors begin to spread through the village that they are having an affair. After the visit to the nurse's house, Emma and Leon go for a walk by the river, during which they feel passionately romantic toward each other.

ANALYSIS: PART TWO, CHAPTERS I–III

The superficiality of Emma's romanticism becomes clear in her interactions with Leon, who shares her love for sentiment and passionate excess. Emma's conversation with Leon at dinner is trite and sentimental—they discuss how books transport them away from their everyday lives—but to the two of them, it seems rapturous and meaningful. She challenges her stable but unsatisfying marriage with a relationship that is based on falsely profound declarations rather than true sentiment.

The birth of Emma's daughter underlines the materialism of her sentiments, but it also introduces some of the novel's feminist arguments. Emma desires to be a maternal figure only when it seems as though the role might be glamorous. As soon as she realizes that she can't buy expensive clothes and furniture for the baby, however, her interest fades, and we see that her only interest in the child is as a vehicle for her own desires. Emma dreams of having a son because she believes that a male child will have the power she lacks. This frank statement shows that Flaubert was aware and perhaps disapproved of the abridged liberties afforded to women in the late nineteenth century. Emma observes that "a man, at least, is free; he can explore all passions and all countries, overcome obstacles, taste of the most distant pleasures. But a woman is always hampered." Emma's lovers always enjoy freedom that she cannot.

Flaubert's description of the mundane world around Emma is realistic, but somewhat exaggerated. He uses flowery, poetic language to describe Yonville, writing that "the country is like a great unfolded mantle with a green velvet cape bordered with a fringe of silver." But Flaubert also recognizes the banality of the setting as "a mongrel land whose language, like its landscape, is without accent or character." By describing the same scene in contrasting ways, Flaubert accomplishes two effects. First, he sets himself apart from his romantic predecessors, who would have appraised a dull scene as unworthy of their attention. Second, he contrasts the banality that Emma sees with the beauty that an outsider might instead perceive. Flaubert thereby establishes that while Emma may be right about the boredom of village life, she is also missing a layer of beauty that her perspective is too narrow to contain.

The villagers who surround Emma provide us with a context for historically understanding Emma's social position. The wet nurse whom Emma visits, for example, lives in a small hut with the children she nurses. When she sees Emma, she begs her for little necessities—a bit of coffee, some soap, some brandy. Although Emma remains unhappy because she can't socialize with the aristocracy in Paris, her visit to the wet nurse reminds us that she is comparatively well-off. The village innkeeper, meanwhile, is a down-to-earth woman whose only concerns are whether the meal will be served on time and whether the drunkards who frequent the inn will destroy the billiards table. Although she does lack imagination, she also represents something that Emma is not: a woman who accepts and enjoys her lot in life.

PART TWO, CHAPTERS IV–VI

> *The fire was out, the clock went on ticking, and
> Emma vaguely wondered at this calm of all things
> while within herself there was such a tumult.*
>
> (See QUOTATIONS, p. 53)

SUMMARY: CHAPTER IV

During the winter, the Bovarys often go to Homais's house on Sunday evenings. Here, Emma and Leon develop a strong rapport. Each feels powerfully attracted to the other, but neither has the courage to admit to the feeling. They exchange little gifts, and the townspeople are sure they are lovers.

SUMMARY: CHAPTER V

Emma watches Leon, Homais, and Charles and decides that her husband is so unremarkable that he disgusts her. She realizes that Leon loves her, and the next time they meet, they both are shy and awkward, unsure of how to proceed. Emma is constantly nervous, and she begins to lose weight. She fancies herself a martyr, unable to give herself to love because of the restrictions of her marriage. She plays the part of the dutiful wife to Charles and brings her daughter, Berthe, back home from the wet nurse. Soon, however, Emma's desire for Leon becomes much stronger than her desire to be virtuous, and she gives way to self-pity. She breaks down in tears, and blames Charles for all of her unhappiness. One day, a shopkeeper named Monsieur Lheureux hints to her that he is a moneylender, in case she should ever need a loan.

SUMMARY: CHAPTER VI

Emma hears the church bells tolling and decides to seek help at the church. The curate, Abbé Bournisien, preoccupied with his own problems and with a group of unruly boys in his catechism class, is oblivious to Emma's deep distress. Soon afterward, in a fit of irritability, Emma pushes Berthe away from her, and the little girl falls and cuts herself. Emma claims that Berthe was playing and that she fell accidentally. Emma is frantic and shaken, but Charles eventually calms her.

Leon decides to go to Paris to study law. He loves Emma, but her sentiments make their romance impossible, and he is utterly bored in Yonville. He is also tempted by romantic adventures he suspects will await him in Paris. When he bids Emma farewell, they are both awkward and quiet, but they are both moved. After he leaves, Charles and Homais discuss the lures and difficulties of city life.

———————————

ANALYSIS: PART TWO, CHAPTERS IV–VI

At the conclusion of Part Two, Chapter IV, we learn more about Leon's feelings for Emma. We discover that he feels shame at his cowardice in not declaring his love for her, that he has written and torn-up a number of love letters, and that he feels frustration that Emma is married. The narrative then shifts to Emma, in contemplation of love:

> As for Emma, she did not ask herself whether she loved him. Love, she thought must come suddenly, with great outbursts and lightnings,— a hurricane of the skies, which sweeps down on life, upsets everything, uproots the will like a leaf and carries away the heart as in an abyss. She did not know that on the terrace of houses the rain makes lakes when the pipes are choked, and she would thus have remained safe in her ignorance when she suddenly discovered a rent in the wall.

Flaubert satirizes the romantic idea of love as an overwhelming transformative force of nature by juxtaposing images of hurricanes and tempests with one of the more mundane effects of weather, water damage. By presenting her discovery of the dent in the wall in an ironic tone of regret, he mocks Emma's lack of practical knowledge, as well as her inability and unwillingness to conceive of the actual. Emma's conflict is contained in this passage. She yearns for unreal romantic ideals and is at first ignorant of and then disappointed by the imperfect realities of life, such as decay.

Emma's struggle with her conscience, as she tries to do her best to become a dutiful wife and mother even as she is tempted by a romance with Leon, ultimately amounts to her indulgence of the romantic role of the martyr. But when she shoves her infant daughter away from her in a fit of annoyance, she can no longer pretend to be a dutiful family woman. She is saved from an infidelity with Leon only by his decision to leave for Paris. The incident with Berthe demonstrates Emma's inability to embrace maternal instincts. Just before she pushes her daughter, she stares at her with disgust, regarding her more as a foreign object—a piece of furniture or an animal—than as her own child.

The conversation between Emma and the priest offers Flaubert a chance to poke fun at the superficial nature of religion among the bourgeoisie. When Emma turns to the priest, she is in real need of help. But the Abbé Bournisien is preoccupied not with spiritual matters but with petty banalities: the rowdiness of his pupils and his daily rounds. When Emma says, "I am suffering," he misunderstands her, and assumes that she is referring to the summer heat. The scene is humorous, but it also criticizes the church sharply, implying that it can only provide surface comforts and cannot minister to Emma's very real spiritual need.

Madame Bovary became so famous in part because of its innovative narrative technique. Flaubert matches his prose style to his narrative subject with remarkable accuracy. When Emma is bored, the text seems to crawl; when she is engaged, it flies. Flaubert widens the symbolic reach of his novel with the development of Homais, a character perfectly conceived to represent all that Flaubert hates about the new bourgeoisie. And he introduces foreshadowing when the sinister Lheureux hints to Emma that he is a moneylender.

PART TWO, CHAPTERS VII–IX

> *"Doesn't this conspiracy of society revolt you? Is there a single sentiment it does not condemn?"*

SUMMARY: CHAPTER VII

After Leon's departure, Emma lapses into her old depression. She is moody, irritable, nervous, and miserable. She constantly dreams of Leon, and wishes that she would have given in to her love for him. In this state, she meets a rich and handsome landowner named Rodolphe Boulanger, who brings a servant to be treated by Charles. During the treatment, Justin, Homais's assistant who is infatuated with Emma, faints from the sight of the blood. As Emma tends to him, Rodolphe is taken by her beauty and begins plotting to seduce her.

SUMMARY: CHAPTER VIII

Yonville is astir with excitement for the annual agricultural fair, a festive, merry event featuring animals on display, speeches, and prizes. One of the prizes goes to an old and timid woman, Catherine Leroux, for fifty-four years of service on the same farm. Rodolphe takes Emma inside the empty town hall to watch the ceremony from the window; when they are alone, he confesses his love for her. The representative of the local prefect arrives and gives a speech about public morality. Rodolphe continues to speak of his love and to urge Emma to return his feelings. She tries to act as she thinks is proper for a married woman but can't resist intertwining her fingers with his.

SUMMARY: CHAPTER IX

For six weeks, Rodolphe avoids Emma, calculating that his absence will make her long for him. When he visits her at last, she is cold to him, but quickly finds herself moved by his romantic language. When Charles arrives, Rodolphe offers to loan Emma a horse to ride. She demurs, but Charles later persuades her to accept the offer. Soon afterward, Emma and Rodolphe go for a ride together. In a beautiful forest glade, he again speaks of his love for her. At last, she gives in, and they make love. When she returns home, she is joyful, feeling that her life has at last become romantic. Emma and Rodolphe quickly begin a full-fledged affair; Emma begins sneaking away from home to see Rodolphe. She acts incautiously, neglecting her duties at home in her obsession for her new lover.

ANALYSIS: PART TWO, CHAPTERS VII–IX

Like the wedding in Part One, Chapter IV, the agricultural fair realistically portrays country life and emphasizes Emma's unhappiness. The farmers at the fair counter Emma's yearning and dissatisfaction with contentment. They experience the fair not as a frivolous provincial charade, but as a genuinely enjoyable occasion. In this regard, Catherine Leroux represents Emma's opposite. Unlike Emma, who can't reside in the same place for more than a week without experiencing a crippling longing for romantic transformation, Catherine Leroux has served for fifty-four years on the same farm.

As a suitor, Rodolphe differs from Leon in terms of experience, and his seduction of Emma succeeds on the strength of his time-honed cunning. While both suitors are fundamentally motivated by erotic desire, Leon is shy, sentimentally romantic, and sexually innocent. In contrast, Rodolphe is aggressive, calculatingly pragmatic, and sexually cynical. Whereas Leon regards Emma as a potential partner in a love of equal terms and views her marriage as an obstacle to that bond, Rodolphe views Emma as sexual prey and her marriage as a convenient excuse for seduction without worry of commitment. Rodolphe infers immediately that Emma yearns to escape the yoke of her marriage and desires a lover. He sets about becoming that lover with ruthless precision.

The context of the fair provides sharp ironic contrast to Rodolphe's skillful seduction of the sentimental Emma. Flaubert cuts back and forth between the scene of the seduction and the speech on morality delivered by the bureaucratic official at the fair. In every instance, the official's pompous words emphasize the insincere passion Rodolphe displays toward Emma. When he tells her he loves her, for example, the official presents a local farmer the award for first prize in manure. As the scene continues, Flaubert heightens the pace by including shorter and shorter segments from each speech, until we hear single sentences intercut with each other.

The irony of public morality contrasted with clandestine infidelity occurs again in Charles's unwitting facilitation of Rodolphe's seduction of his wife. When Rodolphe offers to take her riding, Emma first demurs. But Charles, blind to Rodolphe's intentions and hoping to improve Emma's health with exercise, insists she accept. He even writes to Rodolphe himself to arrange the ride. On the ride, of course, Emma gives herself to Rodolphe for the first time, and Charles becomes the unwitting accomplice to his wife's infidelity.

When Flaubert employs high lyricism to describe Emma as she strides across fields at midnight to rendezvous with her lover, she suddenly becomes a sympathetic character. Emma believes herself to be in love, and her pretensions toward high society recede. It's hard to tell, however, whether her sentimental feelings of love are real or a mere function of Rodolphe's manipulations and higher social status. Emma appears to be ignited with real passion, but we know from her earlier attempts at religious and maternal love that she is rarely serious for long. We also know that Rodolphe is an experienced lover who tosses women aside as soon as he grows bored. This foreshadowing indicates to us that Emma is doomed in this affair, and we sympathize with her approaching disappointment rather than her present elation.

PART TWO, CHAPTERS X–XII

*Emma was just like any other mistress; and the charm
of novelty, falling down slowly like a dress, exposed
only the eternal monotony of passion, always the same
forms and the same language.*

(See QUOTATIONS, p. 54)

SUMMARY: CHAPTER X
Emma and Rodolphe become more cautious, now meeting in the arbor in Emma's garden rather than at Rodolphe's house. Rodolphe quickly begins to tire of her; he finds her romantic idealism exhausting and loses interest in her. He continues the affair solely because of Emma's beauty, but he urges her to act more cautiously. His attentions diminish, and she becomes less sure of his love. A letter from her father prompts a memory of her innocent childhood days. Emma begins to feel guilty and tries to redeem herself through sacrifice. She becomes cold to Rodolphe in order to end the affair, and she tries to force herself to love Charles.

SUMMARY: CHAPTER XI
Homais reads a paper praising a surgical procedure that will cure clubfoot. Under pressure from Emma (who hopes to help Charles's career), Homais, and much of Yonville, the cautious Charles agrees to test this procedure on Hippolyte, a clubfooted servant at the inn. Although Hippolyte is more agile on his crippled leg than some men are on two healthy ones, he is talked into the operation by the

townspeople. The attempt makes Charles a local celebrity—but it fails. Hippolyte's leg develops gangrene and must be amputated. Emma judges Charles incompetent and feels disgusted by him. Although her affair with Rodolphe has slowed down considerably, she renews it now with even more passion than before.

SUMMARY: CHAPTER XII

Emma and Rodolphe's affair begins where it left off. As Emma's dissatisfaction with her marriage becomes even more pronounced, she begins to allude to the possibility of leaving Charles. Lheureux, the merchant and moneylender, begins to coax her into making extravagant and unwise purchases. She goes into debt to buy expensive gifts for her lover. Rodolphe, meanwhile, becomes still more easily annoyed by Emma's romantic sentimentality and begins to lose patience with the affair. By now, Emma has been so careless that the whole town knows about her adultery. When Charles's mother comes for a visit, she guesses it too. She and Emma fight, and Charles convinces Emma to apologize to his mother about the fight. After her apology, Emma is humiliated and begs Rodolphe to take her away. She plans to take Berthe with her. With the secret hope of running away with Rodolphe, she becomes more polite and much less irritable with Charles and his mother. The lovers finalize their plans. They decide that they will leave Yonville separately, then meet in Rouen. However, after a meeting in Emma's garden, Rodolphe talks himself out of the idea.

ANALYSIS: PART TWO, CHAPTERS X–XII

As the affair progresses, it becomes increasingly clear that Rodolphe is interested in Emma solely for the sexual pleasure she affords him, and that Emma's flights of romantic fancy are sorely misplaced. Emma is never able to remain happy in one situation for long, and her guilty attempt to reclaim her moral bearing by sacrificing herself for Charles's career is simply the particular form her inevitable depression takes at this point in the story. When Charles characteristically bungles the operation, having allowed Emma and Homais to talk him into performing an unsound procedure on the crippled Hippolyte, Emma rediscovers her disgust for him and returns gladly to Rodolphe's arms.

The operation on Hippolyte brings to light not only Charles's incompetence, but also the real evil that pride and pretension can perpetrate on simplicity and innocence. Hippolyte is stupid and simple, but he is very able. Homais, on the other hand, is the picture of bourgeois pomposity. He loves to hear himself talk, regardless of the inanity of what he is saying. Combined with Charles's incompetence, Homais's know-it-all behavior invites the horrifying scourge of gangrene followed by the gruesome agony of amputation.

The story of Hippolyte can also be seen as an allegory for Emma's life. By trying to alter a mediocre marital situation, Emma will in the end devastate both her family and their finances—much as the doctors destroy Hippolyte's leg by trying to correct a condition that Hippolyte had previously accepted as part of his life. The nature of that destruction, a long, slow poisoning by gangrene, is similar to the long path of increasing adultery, immorality, and financial irresponsibility that Emma has taken.

By this point, the process of Emma's moral degradation has already begun, in fact. Flaubert writes that Rodolphe has made Emma "into something at once malleable and corrupt." Emma's growing internal corruption is matched by an increased attention to superficial appearances. She pays excessive attention to her physical vanities, perfuming herself, polishing her nails, and buying expensive items from Lheureux. At the same time, she grows more and more brazen in her adultery, and her debt to Lheureux increases. Emma puts both her soul and her finances in hock for the sake of an illicit love affair and a few material possessions. Flaubert forges a strong parallel between Emma's moral and financial situations. In the end, it is her financial situation that undoes her.

PART TWO, CHAPTERS XIII–XV

SUMMARY: CHAPTER XIII

Rodolphe has decided not to elope with Emma. The sexual pleasure she provides, he decides, will not be enough to offset the inconvenience and drain of being constantly in her company. As he contemplates the best way of telling her, he reminisces about his former mistresses. He then writes Emma a letter in which he says that because he loves her so much, he must break off their affair, because all he can offer her is pain. His letter is a fabrication, but he feels it will satisfy Emma and minimize the inconvenience to him of ending the affair. He has the letter delivered to Emma concealed at the bottom of a basket of apricots.

When Emma receives the letter, she is devastated. Reading the letter in the attic, she contemplates throwing herself out the window, but stops when she hears Charles calling her. In her agitated state, she leaves the letter there, forgetting to conceal it. That night, as Charles eats the apricots Rodolphe has sent, Emma sees Rodolphe's carriage drive by on its way out of town, and she faints. She declares that she wants to see no one, not even her daughter. She develops a high fever and remains close to death for the next month and a half. Charles calls in doctors from all over the region, but none of them can cure her. By October, however, Emma begins to recover her health.

Summary: Chapter XIV

Charles has a number of worries. Emma's ill health terrifies him, and his financial situation is becoming increasingly dire. The doctors are very expensive, and when Lheureux presents him with a list of Emma's debts, Charles is forced to borrow the money from Lheureux at very high interest in order to pay them off. Meanwhile, Emma, who believes she has had a religious epiphany during her illness, rediscovers the Catholic fervor of her youth. She prays devoutly and is kinder to both Charles and Berthe. But her religion disappoints her. Although she is as passionately devoted to religious practice as she once was to Rodolphe, she finds it offers her none of the same ecstasies. She maintains her practice and kind demeanor, however, becoming friendly with the villagers, including Justin, who by now is completely in love with her. Other frequent visitors are the tax collector, Binet, who offers advice on uncorking cider bottles, and Homais, who suggests that Charles take Emma to the opera in Rouen. The priest and the pharmacist argue over whether or not the theater is moral—Bournisien claiming that it is irreligious and Homais defending it. Eventually, thinking it will benefit Emma's health, Charles decides to take her to the opera.

Summary: Chapter XV

At the opera, Emma finds herself again embarrassed by Charles's unsophisticated behavior, preoccupied with the desire to seem cosmopolitan and aristocratic. But she enjoys the opera a great deal; it reminds her of the romantic novels of her youth and makes her think about events in her own life. At intermission, she is stunned to hear that Leon is in the crowd. She, Charles, and Leon go to a café. Charles and Leon talk, and Emma is highly impressed by the sophistication Leon has acquired since moving to Paris. Leon begins to ridicule the opera but when he learns that Emma might stay in Rouen in order to see the second half, he praises it rapturously. Charles suggests that Emma stay the next day to see the rest of the opera while he returns to Yonville.

ANALYSIS: PART TWO, CHAPTERS XIII–XV

Throughout the novel, Emma undergoes ethical development cyclically. She tends to switch from romantic indulgence to dissatisfaction, misery, and illness to moral resolve, and then begins the cycle again with a new romantic indulgence. This cycle is evident in her relationship with Rodolphe. After Rodolphe cuts off their affair, she becomes religious. Her insincere piety gives way to romantic yearnings, and when she meets Leon at the opera, she is ready to renew their fledgling romance. This cycle, however, cannot last forever, and when she receives Rodolphe's letter, her suicidal thoughts darkly foreshadow her future. Another element of foreshadowing in this scene is never fully realized, however. Emma discards Rodolphe's note carelessly unconcealed in the attic, but trustworthy Charles never suspects her infidelities, and, even when he later finds the note, he naively reckons it refers to platonic friendship.

Although this emotional cycle may seem like a reason to condemn Emma, her heartbreak and subsequent illness are in some ways a product of the society in which she lives. Rodolphe himself blames the end of their affair on "fate," but Rodolphe does have control over the end of the love affair. As a wealthy man, he has much more power than Emma. As a woman with no way to support herself, Emma can't gain freedom by leaving Charles, nor does she have the means to pursue Rodolphe. Furthermore, Rodolphe's life of ease, combined with his status as a man, allows him great sexual liberty. He has had so many lovers that he is detached and cold. As a result, he can abandon Emma with no great feelings of regret.

The scene in which Rodolphe writes his letter to Emma exemplifies Flaubert's ironic combination of humor and pity. The text of the letter itself is ridiculous, full of high sentiment and exclamation points. In a sense, it is exactly the sort of letter that the maudlin Emma might wish for. But Flaubert emphasizes the insincerity of the words by depicting Rodolphe's thoughts as he composes the letter. For example, when Rodolphe writes, "fate is to blame!" he thinks, "that's a word that always helps." By contrasting self-congratulatory comments like this one with the overblown romanticism of the letter itself, Flaubert heightens the insincerity of Rodolphe's sentiments. At the same time, he points out how deceptive the written word can be, which reflects not only on Rodolphe, but on Flaubert himself in his role as a writer.

Flaubert's awareness of the power of written language to deceive makes him cautious not to imbue his descriptions with too much heavy-handed commentary. As he describes Emma's religious ardor, he writes almost like a reporter, carefully describing actions without venturing any comments on them. But Flaubert makes his thoughts understood even while maintaining an apparently objective tone. By using the technique of juxtaposition—that is, by putting Rodolphe's thoughts beside his words—Flaubert conveys the character's malice and insincerity. Elsewhere he deploys words ironically in unexpected contexts to achieve similarly subtle effects. In the statement, "[Emma] fancied herself seized with the finest Catholic melancholy," the lighthearted words "fancied herself" undermine the seriousness of Emma's emotions, making it clear that Flaubert judges his heroine's sentiments to be somewhat ridiculous. He uses a similar technique later, to let us know that the opera Emma likes so much is really a mediocre production. He writes, "Lucie bravely attacked her cavatina in G major," and with this simple phrase we realize that the singer is no great soprano, but just a chorus girl trying to sing difficult opera.

PART THREE, CHAPTERS I–III

SUMMARY: CHAPTER I

Although Leon has all but forgotten Emma during his time at law school, seeing her again has reawakened his old feelings for her, and he goes to see her in her hotel while Charles is gone the next day. They have an intimate conversation about their discontent with life and the romantic nature of death. Finally, Leon confesses his love and kisses Emma. She refuses him, but he begs for another chance, and they agree to meet at the cathedral the next day. Emma then writes him a letter in which she explains that she cannot be his mistress. The next day, Leon goes to the cathedral at the appointed time, but Emma hangs back, hoping to avoid him and not to fall in love with him again. When she arrives, she gives the letter to Leon, but he does not read it. She takes up the offer of the church's beadle for a tour of the building, but finally Leon pulls her away. They call for a carriage. The driver of the carriage is baffled that they would want to be driven about aimlessly, with all the curtains pulled tight, on such a pleasant day. They drive all day and into the evening, and the only sign of life from inside the carriage is a hand that emerges to throw the torn-up scraps of Emma's letter into the wind.

SUMMARY: CHAPTER II
Emma and Leon have spent so much time in their carriage that Emma has missed the coach back to Yonville. She takes a private cab to catch up with it. When she returns home, she is called urgently to Homais's pharmacy, where Homais is having a massive fight with Justin because Justin has taken the key to a storeroom where arsenic is kept. Homais tells Emma that Charles's father has died. Charles is in mourning, and his mother arrives for a long stay at their house in Yonville, much to Emma's dismay. Lheureux appears with another list of debts and encourages Emma to obtain power of attorney over Charles's finances in order to settle the debts. Charles naively believes his wife when she says that this would be the best approach, so he agrees. He even agrees to send her to Rouen for three days so that Leon can draw up the papers.

SUMMARY: CHAPTER III
In Rouen, Emma and Leon enjoy a passionate three-day "honeymoon," making love in their hotel room, taking a boat out to an island, and romancing under the moonlight. One evening, the boatman tells them that a party of well-to-do young people had used the boat the day before; it turns out that Rodolphe was among them. Emma shudders, but quickly recovers herself, making arrangements for Leon to write to her when she returns to Yonville.

ANALYSIS: PART THREE, CHAPTERS I–III
Emma's new love affair proves the weakness of her recent religious contrition. She abandons the church as soon as a new suitor asserts himself. Emma's attraction to the appearance of romance leads her to accept a superficial version of love, from Leon as well as from Rodolphe. Leon has changed a great deal while in Paris. His flighty romantic sentiments have become dulled by the sophistication of the city, and Flaubert allows us to view affairs from Leon's perspective from time to time to show us the deficiency of Leon's emotions

in relation to Emma's desires. Like Rodolphe, Leon is concerned more with the appearance of his love than with love itself. He often "congratulates himself" on what he believes to be a particularly well-turned romantic phrase or gesture. Rodolphe appears on the scene as a masterfully suave seducer. Leon, on the other hand, despite his high opinion of himself, behaves like an impatient schoolboy. When Emma accepts the beadle's offer of a tour of the church, Leon can't wait to have Emma alone and doesn't even try to conceal his impatience. Emma, however, is blind to Leon's foolishness. She has so little sense of sincerity in a lover that she accepts Leon's playacting as sophistication.

The carriage ride with Leon is one of the most famous scenes in *Madame Bovary* because it illustrates synechdoche, a literary figure in which part of something stands for its entirety. The description of the carriage's movements stands in for a description of Emma and Leon making love, and the panting exhaustion of the carriage driver stands in for the panting exhaustion of the lovers within the carriage. The further the carriage goes, the further we know Emma and Leon have gone, so even Flaubert's long list of the districts they visit contributes to our growing sense of certainty that Emma and Leon are consummating their affair inside the carriage. Finally, the hand thrust forth at the very end of the scene to discard the torn pieces of Emma's letter signals both Emma's sexual climax and the end of all her resolutions.

The emptiness of Emma's devotion to religion is literally demonstrated as Emma passes straight from the church into her lover's arms. The scene in the cathedral, like Emma's consultation with the priest in Part Two, Chapter VI, allows Flaubert to criticize religion. Here, as in that earlier scene, Emma is desperately in need of spiritual guidance—but the man of religion is too concerned with worldly things to lend her the help she needs. In this scene, she accepts the beadle's tour because "with her expiring virtue, she clung to the Virgin, the sculpture, the tombs—to anything." But the beadle's labored descriptions of the statuary do not offer the spiritual succor Emma needs.

The lyricism of Flaubert's prose in this section illustrates the belief of both Emma and Leon that their love affair is fantastically romantic, while ironically communicating the narrator's awareness that the affair is cheap and tawdry. On the one hand, Flaubert uses lyrical, poetic language to capture the mood of his characters, writing of Emma, "at times the shadows of the willows hid her completely; then she reappeared suddenly, like a vision in the moonlight." On the other hand, he maintains a detached irony, writing, "they did not fail to make fine phrases about how melancholical and poetic [the moon] appeared to them." The narrator's use of poetic language to describe Emma is not sarcastic; instead, it conveys both the beauty and the absurdity of the situation. Flaubert is never entirely condescending towards his characters, nor does he ever entirely embrace their naiveté.

PART THREE, CHAPTERS IV–VI

SUMMARY: CHAPTER IV

When Emma returns to Yonville, Leon begins inventing pretexts to visit her there. He neglects both his work and his friends in Rouen. Emma continues to sink deeper into debt to Lheureux and convinces Charles to let her take a weekly piano lesson in Rouen, secretly planning to see Leon on a regular basis.

SUMMARY: CHAPTER V

Every Thursday, Emma travels to Rouen, where she sneaks through back alleys in poor neighborhoods to see her lover. She feels emotionally alive during her time with Leon and is anxious and withdrawn at home, even though she continues to act the part of the dutiful wife. Her relationship with Leon grows more intense with each encounter, and the two begin to view one another as characters in a romantic novel. She develops a familiar routine of going to visit him and returning in the carriage to Yonville. On the road between Rouen and Yonville, she periodically encounters a deformed, blind beggar who terrifies her with his lurid, horrible song. At home, Charles nearly discovers the affair when he meets Emma's alleged piano teacher and finds that the teacher does not know Emma's name. But Emma shows him forged receipts from the lessons, and Charles is easily convinced that nothing untoward has occurred.

As a means of paying her mounting debts, Lheureux convinces Emma, who has power of attorney over Charles's property, to sell him some of Charles's father's estate at a loss. He also talks her into borrowing more and more money. When Charles's mother arrives to look over the accounts, Emma has Lheureux forge a bill for a smaller amount of money than she has actually borrowed. Nonetheless, the elder Madame Bovary burns Emma's power of attorney. Charles, however, soon agrees to sign a new one.

Emma is obsessed with her time with Leon, and with experiencing every kind of romantic pleasure. When she stays overnight with Leon in Rouen without telling Charles, she makes her husband feel foolish for worrying about her. From that moment on, she goes to see Leon whenever she feels like it, and he starts to become annoyed by her demands on his time.

SUMMARY: CHAPTER VI

One day when Emma is scheduled to be in Rouen, Homais pays Leon a visit and monopolizes his time. Emma is left waiting in the hotel room and becomes hysterically angry, accusing Leon of preferring Homais's company to hers. She returns home in a rage, beginning to convince herself that Leon is not the man she thought he was. Emma starts to act domineeringly toward Leon, who reacts with resentment.

A debt collector surprises Emma with a visit, and the sheriff serves a legal notice against her. She borrows more money from Lheureux and begins a desperate campaign to raise money to pay her debts, even pawning many objects from Charles's house in Yonville. All the while, she continues to spend decadently during her time with Leon, forcing him to entertain her opulently and providing him the money to do so. He becomes sick of her petulant extravagance, and she becomes disgusted with his reticence. Each of them is bored with their affair. She begins cavorting with unsavory company, even accompanying some vulgar clerks to a disreputable restaurant after a masquerade ball.

When Emma returns to Yonville after the masquerade, a court order awaits her, demanding that she pay 8,000 francs or lose all her property. She again goes to Lheureux for help, but he refuses to loan her any more money, sending her away. Lheureux hopes to foreclose on Charles's estate and everything the Bovarys own.

ANALYSIS: PART THREE, CHAPTERS IV–VI

The essential superficiality of Emma's connection with Leon compounds the disaster of her financial indiscretions. Once her affair with Leon loses its early glow, Emma loses all sense of proportion and propriety, oscillating between extremes of self-indulgence, self-pity, depression, and guilt. Emma and Leon try to make one another into romantic ideals but fail to connect with each other as real individuals. As these ideals crumble around their actual personalities, they become increasingly disgusted with one another. Emma reacts by seeking pleasure at all costs and in more egregious ways. Her initial desire to be a cosmopolitan aristocrat gives way to a carnal, voracious desire for pleasure, evident in her escapades with vulgar men at unsavory parties. Poor Charles continues to facilitate his wife's infidelity, funding the trips she takes to Rouen on the pretext of taking piano lessons. The blind beggar Emma sometimes encounters between Yonville and Rouen is one of the most terrifying figures in the novel. He is a symbol of Emma's moral wretchedness, and his morbid presence also signals her approaching death.

Emma's financial ruin parallels her moral ruin. Once she obtains the power of attorney over Charles's finances, her destructive qualities spiral further out of control. Emma's attempt to transcend the values of her middle-class existence fails as much out of her own free will as the circumstances in which she lives. Even Flaubert, who initially describes Emma as a victim of circumstance, has begun to judge her unfavorably. Emma's moral corruption, however, remains dependent on the will of the men around her. At the end of Part Three, Chapter V, Leon wonders, "where could she have learnt this corruption so deep and well masked as to be almost unseizable?" The answer is Rodolphe. A man is responsible for even Emma's deepest corruption.

Leon's question at the end of Part Three, Chapter V is a classic example of free indirect discourse, a technique that Flaubert perfected. By this point in the novel, the narrative centers around Emma, but Flaubert at times shows his heroine through the eyes of others. He does not offset Leon's and Charles's thoughts with quotation marks, instead he writes directly the words that pass through their minds. At one point, Charles thinks, "What was the meaning of all these fits of temper?" Flaubert knows the answer, of course, but by using free indirect discourse, he lets us see for a moment how bewildered Charles is by Emma's behavior.

Another of Flaubert's techniques is the contrast between lofty, profound sentiments and mundane, ordinary things. Speaking of Leon's love for Emma, he writes, "he admired the exaltation of her soul and the lace on her petticoat." This contrast between spirituality and materiality discredits the depth of Leon's love. He seems to love blindly, caring as much for Emma's petticoats as for her soul. Flaubert employs a similar technique when he describes Emma and

Leon's weekly trysts in a hotel room. In a virtually identical tone, he describes both the lovers' vows they exchange and the decorations on the mantelpiece. This juxtaposition renders the great other-worldly romance Emma conceives a small and sordid affair.

PART THREE, CHAPTERS VII–VIII

> *[S]he would know well enough how one single glance would reawaken their lost love.*
>
> (See QUOTATIONS, p. 55)

SUMMARY: CHAPTER VII

Officers come to the Bovarys' house to inventory their belongings, which they intend to seize to pay Emma's debts. They leave a guard behind; Emma hides him in the attic to keep the development secret from Charles. She schemes and plans to raise the 8,000 francs. The bankers in Rouen refuse to loan her the money, however, and Leon angrily refuses to steal the money from his employer. However, he does halfheartedly agree to try to raise the money from among his friends and bring it to her in Yonville. Upon her return home, Emma gives her very last five-franc piece to the blind beggar. She finds that a public notice has been posted in Yonville announcing the auction of the Bovarys' belongings.

Emma goes to see the town lawyer, Guillaumin, who agrees to help her in return for sexual favors. Emma angrily refuses his offer and leaves. Charles has still not returned home and has no idea what is transpiring, but all the people of Yonville gossip and wonder what will happen. Two of the townswomen spy from an attic window as Emma goes to see Binet, the tax collector, in the attic where he is amusing himself by making napkin-rings on a lathe. They see Emma beg for more time to pay her taxes, then attempt to seduce Binet. When he rebuffs her, Emma decides to go to Rodolphe, hoping that what she believes is his love for her will enable her to get the money from him by offering herself in return.

SUMMARY: CHAPTER VIII

Rodolphe is indeed aroused by the sight of Emma, but when he realizes the purpose of her visit, he becomes taciturn, and tells her he has no money available. Emma angrily leaves, realizing the full extent of her desperate situation. She goes to Homais's apothecary shop, where she convinces Justin to let her into the cabinet where she knows the arsenic is kept. She eats a big handful of it straight from the bottle, then returns home, feeling at peace. Charles has learned about the auction and searches frantically for Emma. He finds her in bed, and she gives him a letter, ordering him not to open it until the next day.

At first, Emma feels nothing and imagines that she will just fall asleep and die. Then an inky taste fills her mouth, and she becomes violently ill, with a terrible pain in her stomach. Charles opens her letter and reads that she has poisoned herself. He and Homais desperately try to figure out what to do. Homais decides that they must analyze the poison and create an antidote. Emma is kind to Charles and little Berthe. Charles and Homais summon doctors from Rouen, including the famous doctor Larivière, but there is nothing to be done. The priest arrives to give her the sacrament. Charles weeps by Emma's bedside, and Emma also weeps. The last sound she hears is that of the blind beggar singing underneath her window as she dies.

ANALYSIS: PART THREE, CHAPTERS VII–VIII

In the chapters leading up to Emma's death, her financial situation parallels and symbolizes her moral depravity. Her interactions with men throughout the chapters demonstrate her growing moral turpitude. When she visits the lawyer, he treats her as if she were a prostitute. She then flirts with Binet, compromising her dignity even further. Finally, she tries to go back to Rodolphe, essentially willing to sell herself—in direct contrast to her outrage when Guillaumin asked her to do exactly that only a few hours earlier. Flaubert describes her unequivocally as a prostitute, adding only that she is "not in the least conscious of her prostitution." Emma is still able to delude herself with sentimental and romantic ideas—the only difference between selling herself to Guillaumin and to Rodolphe is that Emma can tell herself that Rodolphe loves her.

Although Emma has carefully constructed a romantic fantasy world for herself throughout the novel, financial reality wrenches her, fully and finally, out of her dreams. There is no more hiding from her debt; there is no more eluding the facts of the world around her by seeking refuge in fantasy. Every attempt Emma makes in this section to circumvent or overcome her problems separates her from her dreams and demands that she face up to the ruin she has made of her life. Leon is unable to help. She has no recourse. She is desperate to hide her affairs and her financial indiscretions from Charles. Forced to face the actual consequences of her actions, she decides that she would rather die.

In the world of *Madame Bovary,* a woman's only power over a man is sexual. In this section, men hold all of the financial power. Emma and her maid, Félicité, rack their brains for possible solutions, but in the end, men have the ultimate power to rescue Emma. The only strategies that Emma can employ to pull herself out of ruin depend on her posing as a seductress. Even Emma's death depends on Justin's susceptibility to her wiles. Ultimately, women only can watch the action of men and the world. They themselves are able to influence the world only sexually, and only in a limited way. The townswomen who watch Emma's unsuccessful attempt to seduce Binet embody the status of females as spectators.

Throughout the novel, Emma has been the victim of a string of disappointments with the physical world's failure to fulfill her romantic desires. Her death is her final disappointment. She believes that she will die quietly and romantically, and an "ecstasy of heroism" drives her to eat the arsenic. This "ecstasy" is soon transformed into bodily agony and a stinking mess on the floor, when she vomits, writhes in pain, and begs for the poison to work faster. The fact that the act of poisoning herself is called "eating" associates it with the physical act of consumption that has so disgusted Emma and Charles throughout the book. Emma's lifelong desire to escape the confines of the material world is thus completely destroyed by her death.

Flaubert's realistic description of the material world persists through Emma's death scene, relentlessly suggesting that Emma's romantic world bears no resemblance to reality. Flaubert litters the scene with banal commentary on the furniture and the conversations of the men around Emma. Homais, who stands for bourgeois pomposity and banality, seems entirely oblivious to Emma's final throes of agony. His pompous stupidity is contrasted with Larivière's intelligent simplicity and wit in just a few short phrases. When Homais says, "I wished, doctor, to make an analysis, and *primo* I delicately introduced a tube," the doctor replies, "you would have done better to introduce your fingers into her throat."

Emma's death is firmly grounded in a very realistic description of her society. Although it seems possible in earlier sections that Emma will transcend her class, in this section, Flaubert makes it especially clear that Emma is a member of the bourgeois middle class. She is neither peasant nor wealthy merchant. Flaubert highlights her class position by introducing minor characters with class status both below and above Emma's. The first is Mère Rollet, the nurse whom Emma goes to see in a moment of desperation. Mère Rollet reveals her status as a simple peasant in her ability to tell time by holding her fingers up to the sun. Later, left alone in Mère Rollet's hut, Emma can't figure out what time it is because there is no clock. We see that she is much less a peasant than her nursemaid. At the opposite extreme is Guillaumet, whose splendid house Emma examines in awe when she goes to beg him for money. By including these contrasts at such an important moment in the book, Flaubert stresses that Emma's social class is essential to her situation and the events that befall her.

PART THREE, CHAPTERS IV–XI

> *"Perhaps they loved one another platonically," he told himself.*

SUMMARY: CHAPTER IX
Charles is devastated by Emma's death. He plans an extravagant funeral, with three coffins, and arranges for his wife to be buried in her wedding dress. Homais and Bournisien, the priest, come to watch over the body with Charles; they have an argument about the value of prayer and Charles rages against God. As Emma is being dressed for the funeral, a black liquid pours out of her mouth; later, Charles lifts her veil to look at her face, but utters a cry of horror. He asks Homais to cut away a lock of her hair, and Homais does so, leaving a bald patch in the midst of her hair.

SUMMARY: CHAPTER X
Rouault, having received news that his daughter was ill, arrives in Yonville and discovers that Emma is dead. He attends the funeral along with Charles and the whole town, including Lheureux and Hippolyte, who wears his best false leg for the occasion. Justin does not attend, but visits Emma's grave in the middle of the night to mourn privately.

SUMMARY: CHAPTER XI
One after another of Emma's creditors contacts Charles, demanding payment of a staggering sum of money. Charles attempts to raise it,

but learns that Emma has already collected all the money his patients owe him. He is forced to borrow more and more, and to sell articles from around the house. He continues to idealize his wife's memory. When Leon is engaged to a well-bred young woman, Charles sends him a letter of congratulations, remarking that his wife would have been happy for him. Even when he encounters the letter from Rodolphe that Emma had left in the attic, he assumes that it refers to a platonic affection.

Charles lives alone with his wife's memory. Even Homais becomes less intimate with him, in part because he is too busy waging a campaign to expel the blind beggar from the area. Homais is becoming an increasingly well-respected man who always keeps abreast of the latest developments in politics and medicine.

One day, Charles opens Emma's desk and discovers her letters from Leon and Rodolphe. He is forced to confront the fact that Emma was unfaithful to him. He sinks into gloom and begins to keep even more to himself. He has been forced to sell nearly everything he owns in order to keep Emma's creditors at bay, and his spirit is broken. One day, he goes to Rouen to sell his horse to raise more money, and he meets Rodolphe. They have a drink together. Rodolphe expresses feelings of guilt for his part in Charles's ruin. Charles tells him that he knows the truth, but does not hold a grudge against Rodolphe. He blames fate for Emma's behavior.

The next day, Charles dies in his garden. Everything he owned goes to the creditors, and Berthe is sent to live with his mother. When Charles's mother dies, Berthe is dispatched to an impoverished aunt, and she is forced to work in a cotton mill. Homais, meanwhile, continues to thrive and is eventually awarded the Legion of Honor medal.

ANALYSIS: PART THREE, CHAPTERS IV–XI

The section following Emma's death is largely designed to convey the impact of the consequences Emma evaded in death but brought down on the people she left behind. Charles remains faithful to her memory even when he is consigned to a life of comparative poverty. When he discovers Rodolphe's letter in the attic, he assumes it refers to a platonic friendship. Only Emma's drawer full of letters from her lovers serves as evidence powerful and obvious enough to penetrate his innocent obtuseness. When Charles dies shortly after this revelation, the devastation of the Bovarys is complete. Berthe is forced to live with a lower-class aunt and to work as a common laborer. Emma's aristocratic pretensions have imprisoned her child in a life of poverty and dependence.

Perhaps the most powerful representation of the effect Emma had on the lives of those around her can be observed in Justin, Homais's innocent assistant, whom she forced to play an unwitting part in her death. Our sense of Justin's innocence is heightened by the description of him as a "child" when he weeps on Emma's grave. Leon and Rodolphe sleep in their respective beds, not shedding a tear while Justin sobs "under the weight of an immense sorrow." By comparing Emma's lovers and their shallow, jaded insincerity with the honest involuntary passion of an innocent, Flaubert shows how hollow and bereft of sincere emotion Emma's love affairs have been.

In terms of narrative structure, the final chapter of *Madame Bovary* is symmetrical with the first. Emma is absent from both the first and the last chapters of the book, which focus instead on Charles. Her absence reminds us that life continues without her, reducing her life to just one among many. And, just as the book began not with Charles but with an anonymous third party, it ends with Homais, who has played only an occasional part in all of Emma's dramas. The last sentence of the book describes the honors accorded Homais, that torchbearer of bourgeois mediocrity, reminding us again that *Madame Bovary* is a tragedy of class.

SUMMARY & ANALYSIS

IMPORTANT QUOTATIONS EXPLAINED

1. But it was above all at mealtimes that she could bear it no longer, in that little room on the ground floor, with the smoking stove, the creaking door, the oozing walls, the damp floor-tiles; all the bitterness of life seemed to be served to her on her plate, and, with the steam from the boiled beef, there rose from the depths of her soul other exhalations as it were of disgust. Charles was a slow eater; she would nibble a few hazel-nuts, or else, leaning on her elbow, would amuse herself making marks on the oilcloth with the point of her table-knife.

This passage, from Part One, Chapter IX, illustrates Flaubert's combination of realism and emotional subjectivity. The passage exemplifies realism because it pays attention to tiny details, no matter how unpleasant. On the other hand, the writing maintains a subjective tone in that it leads us to feel Emma's disgust and frustration. The importance of the object world to Emma's thoughts is emphasized by the connections of her soul's exhalations to the steam from the beef. Throughout the book, Flaubert links emotions to objects in just this way. By making emotions inseparable from objects, Flaubert denies Emma her one desire: to escape from the physical world she inhabits and live the life she imagines. Here, we see her trapped among objects that disgust her. Because Flaubert does not let us escape from Emma's environment and forces us to notice all its imperfections, we share Emma's frustration and claustrophobia.

2.   She hoped for a son; he would be strong and dark; she
     would call him George; and this idea of having a male
     child was like an expected revenge for all her
     impotence in the past. A man, at least, is free; he can
     explore all passions and all countries, overcome
     obstacles, taste of the most distant pleasures. But a
     woman is always hampered. Being inert as well as
     pliable, she has against her the weakness of the flesh
     and the inequity of the law. Like the veil held to her
     hat by a ribbon, her will flutters in every breeze; she is
     always drawn by some desire, restrained by some rule
     of conduct.

There are two voices in this passage from Part Two, Chapter III;
one belongs to Emma, the other to the narrator. From "A man, at
least, is free" through "a woman is always hampered," we hear
Emma's thoughts, rendered in free indirect discourse, imbued with
a romantic nature. The rest of the passage, however, is the narrator's commentary and anticipates modern feminist thinking. The
passage claims that a woman is powerless not only over her financial situation, but also over her emotions. A double bind occurs
when a woman's involuntary emotions conflict with inescapable
external circumstances. Her only choice is to behave within the
confines of her fixed station in class and the family. Emma's hopes
for a son represent a reimagination of her own identity. She will
enact her revenge through a male heir with access to opportunities
that have been denied her. In contrast to the "strong, dark" male
avenger envisioned at the start of the passage, the will of a woman
takes the form of a veil tied to a hat by a ribbon, susceptible to the
forces of weather. By looking to his subject, a woman, for a physical detail to use in metaphorical comparison to an abstract con-
cept—her will—Flaubert uses realism to heighten the vivid effect
of his social commentary.

3.   The whitish light of the window-panes was softly wavering. The pieces of furniture seemed more frozen in their places, about to lose themselves in the shadow as in an ocean of darkness. The fire was out, the clock went on ticking, and Emma vaguely wondered at this calm of all things while within herself there was such a tumult.

This passage from Part Two, Chapter VI, describes Emma Bovary's overriding frustration—that the outside world doesn't match up with her inner world. Here, Flaubert's attention to specific details—the clock, the fireplace—allows us to envision Emma's surroundings vividly, so we can more effectively contrast them with her turbulent emotions. In this scene, she has just returned from asking the priest for spiritual guidance. The cleric had seemed utterly unaware of her distress. In this passage, even the objects in the room seem to be ignoring her distress, increasing her feeling of isolation.

QUOTATIONS

4. [Rodolphe] had heard such stuff so many times that
    her words meant very little to him. Emma was just like
    any other mistress; and the charm of novelty, falling
    down slowly like a dress, exposed only the eternal
    monotony of passion, always the same forms and the
    same language. He did not distinguish, this man of
    such great expertise, the differences of sentiment
    beneath the sameness of their expressions. Because he
    had heard such-like phrases murmured to him from
    the lips of the licentious or the venal, he hardly
    believed in hers; you must, he thought, beware of
    turgid speeches masking commonplace passions; as
    though the soul's abundance does not sometimes spill
    over in the most decrepit metaphors, since no one can
    ever give the exact measure of their needs, their ideas,
    their afflictions, and since human speech is like a
    cracked cauldron on which we knock out tunes for
    dancing-bears, when we wish to conjure pity from
    the stars.

QUOTATIONS

Madame Bovary's subtle commentary on the inadequacy of language becomes explicit in this passage from Part Two, Chapter IX. Rodolphe doesn't believe Emma because she is forced to use the same words as others have used to describe a very different sentiment. That the same vocabulary must be employed to communicate varying emotions means that words fail in the description of feelings. The extreme degree of this inadequacy is rendered beautifully in the simile of the cracked cauldron, one of Flaubert's most famous lines. This passage is also a great example of how Flaubert shifts between different perspectives. Through the first part of the passage, we see mostly what Rodolphe sees. In the last part, however, the narrator switches to his own point of view to provide us with an opinion on the nature of language.

5. And besides, should [Rodolphe] hesitate to come to her assistance, she would know well enough how one single glance would reawaken their lost love. So she set out towards La Huchette, unaware that she was hastening to offer what had so angered her a while ago, not in the least conscious of her prostitution.

This passage comes from Part Three, Chapter VII. What angered Emma "a while ago" was the idea that she might sell her sex for money. She has already refused Guillaumin's offers of money in exchange for services of the flesh. Here, however, Flaubert points out that her willingness to rekindle her romance with Rodolphe is no better than prostitution. Her unawareness of the equivalence of the two actions demonstrates the degree of her moral corruption as the novel nears its conclusion. At the same time, her belief that Rodolphe truly loved her enough to help her now is proof of her continued naiveté and self-delusion.

KEY FACTS

FULL TITLE
Madame Bovary

AUTHOR
Gustave Flaubert

TYPE OF WORK
Novel

GENRE
Realist fiction

LANGUAGE
French

TIME AND PLACE WRITTEN
Croisset, France; 1851–1857

DATE OF FIRST PUBLICATION
1857

PUBLISHER
Revue de Paris

NARRATOR
In the first chapter, Charles's classmates narrate as a first-person plural "we." It is unclear whether one person or the whole class is speaking. For the rest of the novel, an omniscient third-person narrator tells the story. Although the narrator appears to be objective, he often makes his opinion felt, especially regarding the ridiculous attempts of his characters' efforts to appear sophisticated.

POINT OF VIEW
The first chapter is told from the perspective of one or all of Charles Bovary's schoolfellows. After that, we see the world through Charles's eyes momentarily before being introduced to Emma. The bulk of the novel recounts events as she experiences them, though always in the third person and sometimes giving us a brief glimpse into someone else's mind. Despite the fact that the narrator limits most of his attention to Emma, however,

there is a fairly even mix of objective observations of her
behavior and subjective accounts of her thoughts and feelings.
Flaubert also often uses free indirect discourse, the narrative
integration of thoughts and feelings without quotation marks or
attribution, to show what his characters are thinking. After
Emma's death, the narration is mostly objective.

TONE

Flaubert's attitude toward his story and his heroine is evenly
divided between sympathy and ironic contempt. We know that
he identified strongly with his heroine because he once said
"Madame Bovary is me." His sympathy for her is evident in the
way he describes her passions and the circumstances that
conspire against her. He is also, however, very much aware of
how ridiculous attempts at sophistication by members of the
bourgeoisie can be, and he portrays many of his characters as
foolish, ridiculous and grotesque.

TENSE

Simple past

SETTING (TIME)

The mid-1800s

SETTING (PLACE)

France, including the towns of Tostes, Yonville, and Rouen

PROTAGONIST

Emma Bovary

MAJOR CONFLICT

Emma wishes for romantic love, wealth, and social status
that she cannot attain because she is married to a middle-
class doctor.

RISING ACTION

Emma begins borrowing money to pay for gifts for her first
lover, Rodolphe. When he leaves her, she falls ill, and her
husband, Charles, borrows even more money to pay for her
care. Emma must now borrow more and more to pay off her
debts and to indulge her extravagant tastes. She takes a second
lover, Leon, but he soon grows tired of her.

CLIMAX

Emma's primary creditor, Lheureux, insists that she pay him back and obtains a court order to seize all her property.

FALLING ACTION

Driven to despair, Emma seeks financial help everywhere, but can find none; she eats a handful of arsenic and dies. After Emma's death, Charles loses everything. He finds out about his wife's infidelities and dies a broken man. Emma's daughter, Berthe, is sent to work in a cotton mill.

THEMES

The inadequacy of language; the powerlessness of women; the shortcomings of the bourgeois class

MOTIFS

Death and illness, windows, eating

SYMBOLS

The blind beggar, dried flowers, the lathe

FORESHADOWING

Emma's financial ruin is foreshadowed as early as the novel's first chapter, when Flaubert introduces the danger of poorly handled finances by describing the incompetent money management of Charles' family members. The appearance of Lheureux, coupled with his early efforts to tempt Emma, foreshadows the eventual nature of her downfall: she will get herself further and further into debt with the moneylender. Emma's romantic disappointments are foreshadowed as well; with both Rodolphe and Leon, we see early on that their feelings for Emma are neither as strong nor as durable as she might wish. Finally, the arsenic with which Emma commits suicide is shown to us six chapters before she ends her life.

KEY FACTS

STUDY QUESTIONS & ESSAY TOPICS

STUDY QUESTIONS

1. *Discuss social class in* Madame Bovary. *Is Emma a sophisticated aristocrat born by mistake into a bourgeois prison, or is she simply a middle-class girl obsessed with a richer life? In the world of the novel, are these distinctions meaningful?*

Class distinctions mean everything in the world of *Madame Bovary*, especially to its heroine. Flaubert makes it clear that Emma is strictly middle-class by providing contrasts to her station in life. Rodolphe and the guests at the Marquis d'Andervilliers's ball represent the wealthy and noble. Emma's wet nurse, Hippolyte, and the blind beggar represent the poor.

Emma is frequently conscious of both those above her station and those below it, and her opinions of those people provide a way of understanding her social station. One of the truly refined characters in the novel is the Marquis d'Andervilliers. When the Marquis invites her to his ball, it is because he knows that she is well-mannered and will not embarrass him. This might be taken as a sign that she really is a sophisticated woman whom circumstance has forced to live a middle-class life. On the other hand, her love for the opera, a genre that is considered by the well-educated to be ridiculous, is a sign that her tastes are coarse. Later, when she has to degrade herself and bargain mercilessly to raise money, her identity as a peasant manifests itself. Flaubert suggests that Emma can't escape her peasant roots, saying that her farm-bred nature reveals itself no matter how sophisticated she tries to appear.

2.   *What role does fate play in Emma's downfall? To what degree does she have power over her own destiny?*

Rodolphe, in his letter breaking off the affair with Emma, claims that "fate is to blame"; later, when Charles meets Rodolphe after Emma's death, he, too, rationalizes that "fate willed it this way." In a sense, they are right. Fate, chance, or, more precisely, matters of social and economic class, certainly do play a role. After all, it is not a function of Emma's will that she was born into a middle-class family; nor is it her fault that her lovers abandon her. It is even possible that her romantic, idealistic nature is a result of fate, and that Emma can't control her actions because she can't control her own identity or her natural inclinations. But there are two other factors that contribute to Emma's downfall. The first is Emma herself—an agent making her own decisions. Emma chooses to marry Charles, she chooses to take lovers, and she chooses to borrow money from Lheureux. She also chooses to commit suicide, proving in a final act that she has power—if only a negative destructive power—over her own life. The second factor that contributes to Emma's downfall is the men around her. Charles's inability to satisfy her creates a real trap for Emma in combination with Rodolphe's jaded heartlessness and Lheureux's greedy scheming. Although she makes her own choices, these men severely limit the options she has at her disposal. Charles and Rodolphe's claim that blaming fate is too easy an excuse, both for Emma and for themselves.

3.   *Compare and contrast Charles and Rodolphe. What
      are their attitudes about love? How does each respond
      to Emma?*

On the surface, Charles and Rodolphe could not be more different. Charles has terrible table manners; Rodolphe is gentlemanly and refined. When Charles declares his love for Emma, he does so awkwardly. He is too shy to speak to her himself, so he talks to her father—but even then he can't articulate his request, and Rouault has to prompt him. When Rodolphe, on the other hand, declares his love, he goes on and on in a flowery speech that he delivers in person. The depth of love conveyed by these two very different confessions is also opposite. Rodolphe has no real love for Emma; to him, she is just a plaything. In contrast, Charles loves her deeply, thinks of her constantly, and forgives her no matter what she does.

Despite their many differences, however, Rodolphe and Charles have one thing in common: they both fall in love with Emma for her physical beauty. Each time we see Emma through their eyes, it is her looks that move them. Even Charles, who truly loves Emma, never looks more deeply than her daily movements around the house: he loves to watch her play the piano or do her embroidery.

SUGGESTED ESSAY TOPICS

1. Discuss the theme of love and romance. How do Emma's unrealized dreams of passionate romance contribute to her unhappiness? Are her romantic expectations attainable, or are they fanciful impossibilities? How do Emma and Leon attempt to make each other into their romantic ideals?

2. To what degree is Emma really capable of love? Is she really in love with Rodolphe and Leon? Does she really love Berthe? Use specific textual examples to support your argument.

3. How is the plot of *Madame Bovary* arranged? Does the novel build suspense leading up to Emma's suicide? Is Emma's cycle of frustration-boredom-illness an effective device for pacing her story, or is it repeated too often?

4. What is Homais's role in the novel? Is he simply a symbol for the bourgeoisie, enabling Flaubert to ridicule its attitudes and values, or does he serve a larger narrative purpose?

5. Discuss Flaubert's prose style. How does he match his prose to the mood of his narrative?

6. Discuss the novel's use of irony. With particular reference to the scene of the fair (Part Two, Chapter VIII), how does Flaubert comment on his story by directing the narration toward peripheral details?

REVIEW & RESOURCES

QUIZ

1. What is Charles Bovary's first wife's name?

    A. Heloise
    B. Félicité
    C. Emma
    D. Léocadie

2. How does Emma Bovary kill herself?

    A. She throws herself under an oncoming train
    B. She eats arsenic
    C. She throws herself out the attic window
    D. Her lovers bore her to death

3. How does Charles get to know Emma's father?

    A. In medical school
    B. At an agricultural fair
    C. Charles's first wife is close friends with Emma's father
    D. Charles repairs Emma's father's broken leg

4. How does Emma's father signal to Charles that Emma has accepted his proposal?

    A. By letter
    B. By hanging a white sheet from the gatepost
    C. By slamming a shutter against the wall
    D. By sending him a turkey

5. How does Rodolphe conceal the letter in which he breaks up with Emma?

    A. Under the saddle of his horse
    B. In a basket of apricots
    C. In his underwear
    D. In a bouquet of white lilies

6. When the Marquis d'Andervilliers's ballroom becomes too hot, how do the servants cool it down?

    A. By fanning the guests with peacock feathers
    B. By spraying the guests with water
    C. By breaking the windows
    D. By moving the party outside

7. What item does the Viscount drop that Emma saves to fantasize about?

    A. His cigar case
    B. His riding crop
    C. His opium pipe
    D. His dancing card

8. What is Monsieur Binet's hobby?

    A. Going to the opera
    B. Making napkin rings
    C. Reading romance novels
    D. Amateur medicine

9. In what way is Hippolyte crippled before Charles tries to operate on him and ends up having to perform an amputation?

    A. He is clubfooted
    B. He has syphillus
    C. He is blind
    D. He has gout

10. Where was Emma educated?

    A. In the village school at Tostes
    B. In Paris
    C. In a convent in Rouen
    D. At home

11. Where do Leon and Emma make love for the first time?

    A. On the garden seat at the Bovarys' house
    B. In Leon's office
    C. In a carriage
    D. In a hotel room in Rouen

12. Where do Emma and Rodolphe make love for the first time?

    A. On Charles's desk
    B. In Rodolphe's mansion
    C. In the woods
    D. In a boat

13. Where does Rodolphe declare his love for Emma?

    A. At an agricultural fair
    B. At the Marquis d'Andervilliers's ball
    C. At the opera
    D. Through her window

14. Who is Catherine Leroux?

    A. Emma's first servant, whom she dismisses
    B. An old woman who is rewarded for her loyal service on a farm
    C. The wet nurse who looks after Emma's daughter
    D. Leon's other lover, whom he later marries

15. What eventually happens to Emma's daughter?

    A. She goes to work in a cotton mill
    B. She is sold into prostitution by Lheureux
    C. She marries well and abandons her father
    D. She seeks revenge on Rodolphe

16. What important document does Emma obtain from her husband?

    A. His will
    B. His dead wife's will
    C. A writ of habeas corpus
    D. A power of attorney

REVIEW & RESOURCES

17. What lie does Emma tell in order to go visit Leon each week in Rouen?

    A. She has a job there selling flowers
    B. She needs to go to confession
    C. She is taking piano lessons
    D. She is going to visit her father

18. Where does Charles find the letter from Rodolphe that broke off the affair with Emma?

    A.　In the attic
    B.　In her desk
    C.　Hidden under a statue in the garden
    D.　In the kitchen behind the stove

19. When Charles and Emma get married, where do they go for their honeymoon?

    A.　Switzerland
    B.　Scotland
    C.　Tostes
    D.　Rouen

20. To what other use does the gravedigger, Lestiboudois, put his graveyard?

    A.　He gives tours of the ancient graves
    B.　He brings his mistresses there
    C.　He holds séances there
    D.　He grows potatoes there

21. Why can't Emma marry Charles immediately after he proposes?

    A.　He is still in mourning for his first wife
    B.　He is still married to his first wife
    C.　He still hasn't completed medical school
    D.　Her father forbids it

22. Apart from the effect it has on her health, what is the consequence of Emma's illness after Rodolphe leaves her?

    A. It causes Rodolphe to change his mind and come back to her
    B. It makes Charles realize that she is having an affair
    C. It drives the Bovarys deeper into debt
    D. It kills her unborn child

23. How many extramarital affairs does Emma have?

    A. None
    B. One
    C. Two
    D. Four

24. What impressive credential does the old man at the Marquis d'Andervilliers's ball have?

    A. He personally baked all the cakes for the party
    B. He once slept with Marie Antoinette
    C. He fathered seventeen children
    D. He owns an entire province

25. Where does *Madame Bovary* open?

    A. On the farm where Emma grew up
    B. In Charles's grade-school classroom
    C. In Flaubert's living room
    D. At the Bovarys' dinner table

ANSWER KEY:
1: A; 2: B; 3: D; 4: C; 5: B; 6: C; 7: A; 8: B; 9: A; 10: C;
11: C; 12: C; 13: A; 14: B; 15: A; 16: D; 17: C; 18: A; 19: C;
20: D; 21: A; 22: C; 23: C; 24: B; 25: B

SUGGESTIONS FOR FURTHER READING

BARNES, JULIAN. *Flaubert's Parrot.* New York: Vintage Books, 1990.

BLOOM, HAROLD, ed. *Modern Critical Interpretations: Gustave Flaubert's* MADAME BOVARY. New York: Chelsea House Publishers, 1988.

FLAUBERT, GUSTAVE. *Madame Bovary: Backgrounds and Sources; Essays in Criticism.* Ed. and trans. Paul de Man. New York: W.W. Norton & Company, 1965.

GANS, ERIC. MADAME BOVARY: *The End of Romance.* Boston: Twayne Publishers, 1989.

HEATH, STEPHEN. *Gustave Flaubert:* MADAME BOVARY. New York: Cambridge University Press, 1992.

SARTRE, JEAN-PAUL. *The Family Idiot: Gustave Flaubert, 1821–1857.* Trans. Carol Cosman. Chicago: University of Chicago Press, 1981.

STEEGMULLER, FRANCIS, ed. *The Letters of Gustave Flaubert.* Cambridge: Harvard University Press, 1982.

A Note on the Type

The typeface used in SparkNotes study guides is Sabon, created by master typographer Jan Tschichold in 1964. Tschichold revolutionized the field of graphic design twice: first with his use of asymmetrical layouts and sanserif type in the 1930s when he was affiliated with the Bauhaus, then by abandoning assymetry and calling for a return to the classic ideals of design. Sabon, his only extant typeface, is emblematic of his latter program: Tschichold's design is a recreation of the types made by Claude Garamond, the great French typographer of the Renaissance, and his contemporary Robert Granjon. Fittingly, it is named for Garamond's apprentice, Jacques Sabon.

SPARKNOTES
TEST PREPARATION
GUIDES

The SparkNotes team figured it was time to cut standardized tests down to size. We've studied the tests for you, so that SparkNotes test prep guides are:

Smarter:
Packed with critical-thinking skills and test-
taking strategies that will improve your score.

Better:
Fully up to date, covering all new features of the tests,
with study tips on every type of question.

Faster:
Our books cover exactly what you need to
know for the test. No more, no less.

SparkNotes Study Guides: